THOMAS COOK
Travellers

KU-545-677

CALIFORNIA

BY
ROBERT HOLMES

Produced by AA Publishing

Written by Robert Holmes

Original photography by Robert Holmes

Edited, designed and produced by AA Publishing. Maps © The Automobile Association 1995

Distributed in the United Kingdom by AA Publishing, Norfolk House, Priestley Road, Basingstoke, Hampshire RG24 9NY.

The contents of this publication are believed correct at the time of printing. Nevertheless, the publishers cannot accept responsibility for any errors or omissions, or for changes in the details given in this guide or for the consequences of any reliance on the information provided by the same. Assessments of attractions, hotels, restaurants and so forth are based upon the author's own experience and, therefore, descriptions given in this guide necessarily contain an element of subjective opinion which may not reflect the publishers' opinion or dictate a reader's own experiences on another occasion.

We have tried to ensure accuracy in this guide, but things do change and we would be grateful if readers would advise us of any inaccuracies they may encounter.

First published 1993
Revised second edition © The Automobile Association 1995
Reprinted 1997
Reprinted June 1998

© The Automobile Association 1995

All rights reserved. No part of this publication may be reproduced, stored in a retrieval system, or transmitted in any form or by any means – electronic, photocopying, recording, or otherwise – unless the written permission of the publishers has been obtained beforehand. This book may not be lent, resold, hired out or otherwise disposed of by way of trade in any form of binding or cover other than that in which it is published, without prior consent of the publisher.

A CIP catalogue record for this book is available from the British Library.

ISBN 0 7495 0947 3

Published by AA Publishing (a trading name of Automobile Association Developments Limited, whose registered office is Norfolk House, Priestley Road, Basingstoke, Hampshire RG24 9NY. Registered number 1878835) and the Thomas Cook Group Ltd.

Colour separation: BTB Colour Reproduction, Whitchurch, Hampshire

Printed by Edicoes ASA, Oporto, Portugal

Cover picture: *San Francisco's Golden Gate Bridge*
Title page: *The Embarcadero Center, San Diego*
Above: *San Francisco skyline*

Contents

Introduction

*T*he 'Golden State' of California is one of the best-known areas on earth, if not from personal experience then vicariously through the media and movies.

The history is remarkable. In only 150 years, it has grown from a wilderness of desert and mountains to be the world leader in high technology. It has the sixth largest gross national product in the world, and each year it adds another 600,000 to its population.

It is the state where dreams are made and broken. It is the state where movie stars can become presidents. Anything is possible in California, or so it seems. California is still the land of dreams but for some those dreams are turning into nightmares. The global downturn in the economy has also had its effect on California, and unemployment is at its highest since the Great Depression. Businesses are closing and going into bankruptcy with alarming frequency, and even the most established names may no longer be around by the time this book is published.

Budget cutbacks are curtailing many

Fisherman's Wharf, San Francisco

San Francisco specialities

things, including the opening hours at many attractions, and it is wise to check before any visit. At the time of writing, however, all the information given in this book was correct.

This guide is an attempt to give as complete a picture of the state as possible with enough practical information to enable visitors to make the most of their time here. California has more to offer than any other state in the Union and it can take a lifetime to see it all. Try not to do too much on a first visit, take it slowly, and let California work its magic.

CALIFORNIA QUOTES

'All scenery in California requires distance to give it its highest charm.' Mark Twain 1872

'I am usually very calm over the displays of nature, but you will scarce believe how my heart leaped at this. It was like meeting one's wife. I had come home again.' Robert Louis Stevenson, 1879

'...the various landscapes of California – Switzerland and Burgundy and Yorkshire and Scotland and Spain.' Alistair Cooke, 1973

'When a tree takes a notion to grow in California nothing in heaven or on earth will stop it.' Lillian Leland, 1890

'East is East, and West is San Francisco ... Californians are a race of people; they are not merely inhabitants of a state.' O Henry 1910

'California is a wonderful place to live – if you're an orange.' Fred Allen

'The attraction and superiority of California are in its days. It has better days, and more of them, than any other county.' R W Emerson, 1871

'I attended a dinner the other morning given for the Old Settlers of California. No one was allowed to attend unless he had been in the State two and one-half years.' Will Rogers, 1924

'Southern California, I found, is a veritable paradise of statuspheres.' Tom Wolfe

'California is the only state in the Union where you can fall asleep under a rose bush in full bloom and freeze to death.' W C Fields

'California, more than any other part of the Union, is a country by itself, and San Francisco a capital.' James Bryce, 1901

'The coldest winter I ever spent was a summer in San Francisco.' Mark Twain

THOMAS COOK CALIFORNIA

California became a popular destination for the Thomas Cook travellers as soon as the company opened up the USA to British travellers. Cook's first round-the-world tour of 1872–73 took in California, and in 1876 the company ran the first tour to California in its own right. The journey was by Pullman Cars on the transcontinental railroad from the eastern ports – a distance of 3,000 miles to Merced, California, where passengers transferred to stagecoach to visit Yosemite Valley (which had become part of the world's first National Park in 1864). Tourists explored Yosemite by stagecoach or in the saddle, before rejoining the train to San Francisco for four days' sightseeing. All the elements of a present-day escorted tour of California were already there in Cook's inaugural 1876 expedition – even visits to the Napa Valley vineyards. Only Los Angeles, which began to grow in the 1880s, and Disneyland, which came much later, were not included.

History

1500
California is inhabited by 105 native American tribes speaking more than 100 dialects

1542
Juan Rodríguez Cabrillo discovers San Diego Bay while on an expedition to the north looking for gold and spices

1579
Francis Drake, before his knighthood, reputedly lands to the north of San Francisco in the *Golden Hind* and claims the territory for England, naming it Nova Albion

1769
Father Junípero Serra and Juan Gaspar de Portolá establish the first permanent European settlement in San Diego. El Camino Real is built along the route of present-day Highway 101

The Gold Rush of 1849

1776
Franciscans establish the Mission Dolores, the first settlement of San Francisco. The same year Juan Bautista de Anza reaches San Francisco at the head of the Mexican overland expedition

1781
Spanish families establish Los Angeles with 41 settlers

1812
Russians build a trading post at Fort Ross near Bodega Bay

1821
Mexico attains independence from Spain

1822
California declares allegiance to the newly independent Mexico

1826
Overland arrival of Jedediah Smith from across the Sierra Nevada signals the beginning of the US migration westward

1846
US settlers attempt the unsuccessful 'Bear Flag Revolt'

1848
Mexico cedes California to the US following the Mexican–American war. James Marshall discovers gold while constructing a saw mill by the American River

1849
Gold rush increases population of San Francisco to 24,000

1850
California becomes the 23rd state of the Union. The first capital is San Jose

1854
Sacramento becomes the 4th and final capital of the state

1869
First transcontinental link between the

Devastation in Compton from the 1933
earthquake – that of 1906 was even worse

east and west coasts established with the
link of Central Pacific and Union Pacific
railroads
1873
First cable cars run in San Francisco
1890
Congress establishes Yosemite National
Park
1906
The great earthquake and fire in San
Francisco
First film studio opens in Los Angeles
1915
Pan Pacific Exhibition in San Francisco
1920
Population of Los Angeles overtakes San
Francisco at 576,673
1930
Dust Bowl refugees arrive from the
Midwest
1932
Olympic Games held in Los Angeles
1937
Golden Gate Bridge is completed
1945
United Nations Organisation founded in
San Francisco
1955
Disneyland opens in Anaheim
1967
Ronald Reagan elected as Governor.
San Francisco becomes centre of the
hippy movement
1984
Olympic Games held in Los Angeles
1989
Worst earthquake in San Francisco
since 1906
1993
6.8 magnitude Northridge earthquake
disrupts Los Angeles

Geography

*I*n many ways California has more similarities to a country than to a state. It is big. Of the 50 states only Alaska and Texas are bigger. The coastline stretches for 1,265 miles from the mist-shrouded redwood forests on the Oregon border to the hot, dry deserts of Mexico, and it is the most fertile state in the Union.

Yet in spite of its size, most of the 28 million population chose life on the geological fault line, or more accurately on a series of fault lines, extending along the whole coastal region, including the infamous San Andreas Fault passing through San Francisco.

California can conveniently be divided in two with San Francisco as the hub for northern California and Los Angeles for the southern part of the state. The majority of visitors will fly into one of these hub cities.

The most northerly part of the state, bordering Oregon, is a wilderness of lakes and forests. For the fisherman, hunter, birdwatcher or hiker there is enough territory to explore to last a lifetime. On the northern coast, giant redwoods have been the basis of a timber industry that has provided the main economy for the region.

Further inland, the seismic nature of the state is dramatically evidenced in the moon-like landscape of Lava Beds National Monument and the two volcanoes that are at the end of the chain that includes Mount St Helens in Washington. Mount Shasta, with its five permanent glaciers, rises to 14,170 feet above the lake of the same name. The southernmost link in the chain is 10,460-foot Lassen Peak which had its last major eruption in 1915 and now forms the basis of Lassen National Park.

California is still a landscape under construction and its situation on the junction of two tectonic plates has resulted in some of the most dramatic and contrasting scenery in North America. At 14,495 feet, Mount Whitney is the highest mountain outside Alaska and is a mere 90 miles from Bad Water which, at 282 feet below sea level, is the lowest elevation in the western hemisphere. California has three mountain ranges, three desert systems, thousands of lakes, and forests where you can find not only the tallest trees in the world but also the oldest and the largest.

On the eastern border of the state with Nevada at 6,000 feet above sea level lies Lake Tahoe, covering an area of 200 square miles and surrounded by the mountains of the Sierra Nevada. Every winter, this is the centre for Olympic-class skiing at resorts such as Squaw Valley. In the summer it is a hikers' paradise.

The Sierra Nevada mountains stretch 400 miles south from Tahoe. They were created 10 million years ago by tremendous forces after the oceanic plate began undercutting the continental plate to form California. Two million years ago glaciers carved out the spectacular valleys and granite domes for which the Sierra is famous. Apart from being the highest mountain range in continental United States, it is one of the fastest growing on earth, rising at a rate of 2 inches a year.

The Sierra Nevada forms the eastern boundary of the central valley which is one of the most fertile and productive agricultural areas of the nation. Long, dry summers and wet winters, together with rich alluvial soil, make the valley ideal for large-scale crop farming, growing everything from cotton to grapes.

San Francisco Bay is the largest natural harbour on the West Coast, and the coastal area from the city of San Francisco down to San Diego is the most heavily populated part of the state.

Sonoma and Napa to the north of San Francisco down as far as Santa Barbara in the south provide locations with the perfect combination of soil type and climate to produce some of the world's best wines.

Southern California is dominated by the Los Angeles conurbation with a 3.5-million population. Urban sprawl and freeways extend from Santa Monica down as far as Newport Beach and inland to San Bernardino, an area bigger than some east coast states. The coastal highway continues south to San Diego, California's first settlement and now its second largest city with a population of 1,130,000. Beyond San Diego lies Mexico.

To the east of all this urban development is desert. The desert starts where the Sierra Nevada mountains and the central valley end and continues down into Mexico and across to Arizona and New Mexico. Three great desert systems, the Mojave, Colorado and Great Basin, combine to form part of the world's third largest arid region. This is the land of the cactus and sage brush, sand dunes, and some of the highest recorded temperatures on earth. A shade temperature of 134°F has been recorded in Death Valley.

Stovepipe Wells dunes, Death Valley

Politics

*I*n California, politics has become a struggle not of men but of forces. Once seen as an abundant and promised land, the Golden State in recent years has come up against severe limits. Drought, runaway growth, economic deficits, pollution and a host of other factors have combined to push the state up against the wall. Yet there remains in California politics a dream that fuels life here on the edge of the continent, and gives birth to the trends and tastes of America.

The main political battleground is the state capital of Sacramento. As a centre of government in the United States, Sacramento is second only to Washington, D C. It is the training ground of US congressmen, presidents and Supreme Court justices, and the home of innovative government policy.

California also plays a crucial role in national politics. The state sends more legislators to the US House of Representatives and the US Senate than any other. It is the biggest prize in presidential elections as well, giving the winner 54 electoral votes – 20 per cent of the total electoral votes needed to win a presidential election.

Inspite of California's liberal reputation there has been a succession of conservative Republican governors, including, of course, Ronald Regan. In recent years both environmental and especially economic problems have grown to gigantic proportions. Pete Wilson inherited an unenviable challenge when he was elected governor in 1990. A former US senator, Mayor of San Diego and Republican, Wilson is nevertheless a moderate who has battled to find solutions to the ever growing problems.

The issues being played out in California today are the issues facing America tomorrow. Among them are:

Welfare reform: California, like America, faces a government deficit growing at an alarming rate. Drastic measures are being sought to bring this runaway fiscal situation under control. The position was so serious in mid-1992 that the state could only make payments in IOUs. It was virtually bankrupt. Naturally, debate is heated between the conservative Republicans and the more liberal Democrats.

Growth management: Statewide plans are being prepared to control the

Democratic Party Convention, San Francisco – fun atmosphere but serious politics

Smog descends on downtown Los Angeles

relentless sprawl of suburban development that is gobbling up land in California's central valley, and on the outskirts of Los Angeles, San Francisco and Sacramento. One of the nations first growth management plans was in San Diego during Pete Wilson's term as mayor.

Environmental issues: In the Los Angeles Basin, eight million vehicles along with manufacturing plants help to produce the nation's dirtiest air. In the Sacramento River Delta, water diversions have damaged one of the West Coast's most important estuaries and have pushed several species perilously close to extinction. Along California's north coast, a 'timber war' has broken out between environmentalists and timber companies over the cutting of some of the state's last remaining redwood trees. These and other issues will dominate politics in the state that brought the world Earth Day.

Changing demographics: To drive California's streets is to see America's ethnic future. People from every nation in the world populate its towns and cities. This rich multicultural mix, however, is a mixed blessing. The state is seeing an exodus of people in their productive years, while more and more immigrants are children. From schools to offices, Californians are struggling to meet the needs of newcomers and keep the state's economy strong. As California enters the 1990s, there is a growing dissatisfaction with the direction the state is headed and with the state's leadership. In 1991, voters in San Francisco turned out the incumbent mayor, Art Agnos. But that was the exception. Despite a rise in voter resentment, the *status quo* still dominates California politics.

Oil drilling – an environmental hazard off the beautiful Santa Barbara coast

Culture

*O*f all the states in the nation none is more culturally diverse than California. Although Sir Francis Drake reputedly landed at Point Reyes in 1579, a few miles north of San Francisco, the first European settlers were the Spanish, who initially explored the southern coast and then moved up from Mexico to establish their chain of missions.

In the mid-1800s a massive influx of European immigrants made their way from the East Coast in search of gold. This gave a strong European base to the population, which still exists today.

Almost 25 per cent of the population is Hispanic with the majority of these coming from neighbouring Mexico but also including Cubans, Puerto Ricans and various Central Americans. This figure does not include the thousands of illegal immigrants that continue to cross the Mexican–US border.

The massive Californian agricultural industry could not survive without this tremendous pool of labour. These immigrants, who enter the US daily both legally and illegally, provide low-wage labour, not only for agriculture but in factories and the service industries. They traditionally fill the jobs that other Californians refuse to take.

Behind this new influx of immigrants is an Hispanic establishment whose families have been in California for generations. They are business owners, Congressmen and leaders in local politics throughout the state.

The Hispanic population tends to settle in neighbourhoods. East Los Angeles is 90 per cent Latino and the largest Hispanic community in the US. In San Francisco it is the Mission District. In the central valley towns over a third of the population is Hispanic.

Every year on 5 May, Mexican Independence Day, the Latin-American culture throughout California explodes into festivals of song, dance and music that rival Carnival in their exuberance. The Cinco de Mayo celebrations attract over 150,000 participants in both San Francisco and San Jose alone.

The oriental influx started as early as 1850 when Chinese railroad workers followed the Gold Rush and started to develop their now world-famous Chinatown in San Francisco. During the following decade Japanese immigrants started to arrive at Gold Hill in El Dorado County.

In the 1970s California was a major centre for relocating Southeast Asian refugees. By 1980 there were 19 separate Asian groups in the state, the six largest being Chinese, Filipino, Japanese, Asian-Indian, Korean and Vietnamese. Between 1980 and 1990 California's Asian population almost doubled to 2.3

Chinatown Lion

will represent about 11 per cent of the population.

California's position as a Pacific Rim trading and banking power has helped to consolidate the state's position as an Asian stronghold.

The Asians have made their most obvious mark through the multitude of restaurants throughout the state.

The Asians generally remain low key and quietly make their mark without any fuss. Among those who have succeeded in the arts are San Francisco author Amy Tan who won the 1989 National Book Award and Stanford graduate David Henry Hwang who won the Tony Award for his play *M Butterfly*. The black population in California is far less significant than in many eastern states, partially due to the lack of slavery on the West Coast.

The only non-immigrant residents are the Native Americans, and over 1 million make their home in the Golden State – the largest population of any state. They have lived there for over 10,000 years.

California's rich cultural diversity is a major element in the state's charm.

million people. This latest influx has also been from Southeast Asia and the newcomers are Laotians, Cambodians and Hmong. By the year 2000 it is expected to increase by a further 50 per cent by which time Asian-Americans

Faces of California

First Steps

California is in many ways as familiar as our own backyards. You see it on television, you see it in films, and magazines are always featuring the latest California trends.

Oakland Bay Bridge

DRIVING

For most visitors the first contact comes after picking up a rental car at the airport. Will the streets be full of budding Steve McQueens screeching round corners at 90mph? Far from it. Driving on the right may be confusing and the freeway traffic may appear intimidating but no one goes very fast. All urban freeways have a maximum speed limit of 55mph and most people adhere to this. Generally you can drive at 5mph over the limit without worrying about speeding tickets, but you cannot completely guarantee it.

The most disturbing aspect of freeway travel is that people overtake on all sides. Theoretically there is a fast lane but it is not unusual to find someone in it pottering along at 40mph. Fortunately lane discipline is very good, but remember to keep you eyes open and use your mirrors frequently.

Rural freeways have a 65mph limit. Speed limits will be clearly posted so there should not be any confusion.

Speeding tickets are fairly expensive, so take care. Black and white California Highway Patrol cars operate on the freeways, and in towns and cities radar traps are frequently used. Drink-driving laws are extremely tough so do not even take a chance.

PARKING

Although, or maybe because, the car is such a major part of life in California, looking for a parking space, particularly in city centres, can be like the search for the Holy Grail.

Street parking is generally regulated by meters with time limits ranging from 15 minutes to 4 hours. The majority of meters allow 1 hour parking and they almost all accept 25 cent coins. Feeding meters is prohibited but it is a common practice nevertheless.

If a meter is obviously broken the usual solution is to write 'Meter Broken' on a paper grocery bag and place it over the meter. This will usually prevent a parking ticket.

Always read notices attached to meters. On major streets in cities parking is often restricted at peak commute times; 7am to 9am and 4pm to 6pm are the most common hours and during this period you will not only get a hefty parking ticket, but also have your car towed at considerable additional expense, not to mention inconvenience.

In business districts some meters will be allocated specifically for commercial vehicles. This will be clearly stated on both the meter and the curb. Parking restrictions are indicated by curb side colour codes. Red means no parking at any time, day or night. White indicates a drop-off and pick up zone, usually seen in front of hotels, restaurants and hospitals. Cars cannot be left unattended in this zone. Yellow is strictly for commercial vehicles and is normally only enforced during business hours. The hours will always be posted on the curb. Blue indicates a handicapped zone that is permanently reserved for cars displaying a special handicapped plaque. Certain meters displaying a wheelchair symbol are also exclusively reserved for handicapped motorists. Never, ever park in blue zones. They carry the highest parking penalty.

All streets without meters or colour codes are available for parking unless otherwise posted, but remember to always park in the direction of the traffic.

In most towns, parking is prohibited for a couple of hours one day of the week for street cleaning. This can be almost any time of the day or night so always read the small print on street signs.

Follow the San Andreas earthquake trail at Point Reyes

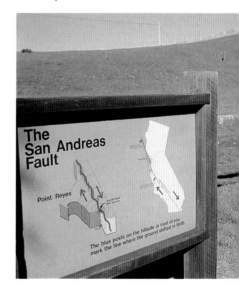

STREETS OF GOLD

Is this sun-drenched land of milk and honey all that it appears? What is the reality behind the myth?

Many myths have been built on the California riches and lifestyle that can seem to be so alluring from the frozen climates of the north. People have been attracted to California in search of these myths in huge numbers since the discovery of gold in 1848. Since then, the population has doubled every 20 years.

Spain and Mexico ruled California for almost 80 years without finding the large deposits of gold that they thought existed. It was finally discovered in 1848 by John Marshall just days before Mexico transferred California to the United States, which paid $18.25 million for California along with Utah, Nevada, Arizona, New Mexico and even parts of Texas and Colorado. Within 10 years, 30 times that amount had been mined from the newly-found mines.

California is still a relatively rich state but the global recession of recent years has certainly had an impact. There is an increasing homeless problem in the big cities and panhandlers begging on street corners are a common sight in all but the most affluent areas.

FOOD

In one sense California is certainly the land of plenty. The central valley is one of the world's most productive agricultural regions and the shelves of any supermarket will reflect the wealth of fresh produce available. An impressive range of fruits and vegetables are grown there and most of them are available year round at inexpensive prices. Grapes are a major crop, and some of the world's finest wines flow from bottles produced in the Napa Valley.

Inevitably a whole culinary trend has grown around this foundation and California cuisine has become synonymous with the finest in modern gastronomy. Even in the most modest restaurants the food will generally be

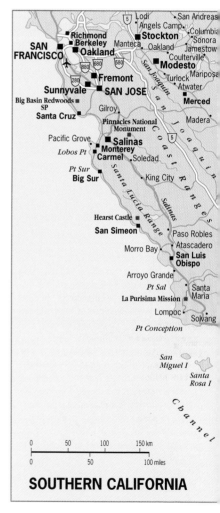

SOUTHERN CALIFORNIA

good, and certainly plentiful. Service is always of a polite and highly efficient level, the expectation of a tip doing much to promote this atitude.

WHEN TO GO

If you are travelling with children the best months are June, July and August when Disneyland is at its busiest. If you are looking for a quieter time March, April, May, then late September, October and November are more peaceful and avoid the period when local Americans take their holidays.

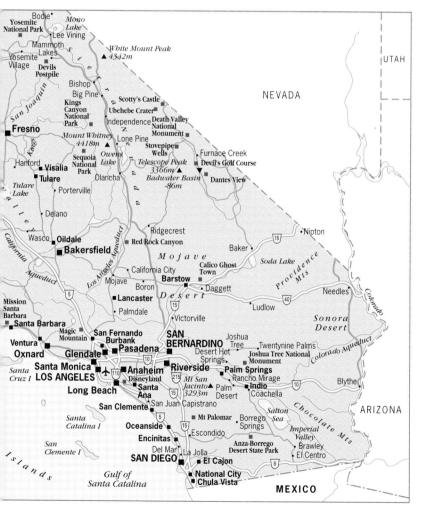

SHOPPING

Service standards are generally high and there is a strong work ethic. Shops are open late and some shops never close. Most major supermarkets, where you can buy anything from light bulbs to whiskey, are open until at least 10pm and often until midnight. The 7–11 chain of convenience stores never close at all, 365 days of the year, and they can be found in most towns. They stock a basic range of foodstuffs and also serve coffee and some fast foods.

Even the big department stores open late at least one night a week and all but the smallest shops are open on Sundays. Sales are a way of life here and most weeks one store or another will have one. The prices can sometimes be unbelievably low and, depending upon foreign exchange rates, there are some incredible bargains to be found. Local newspapers always carry advertisements with details.

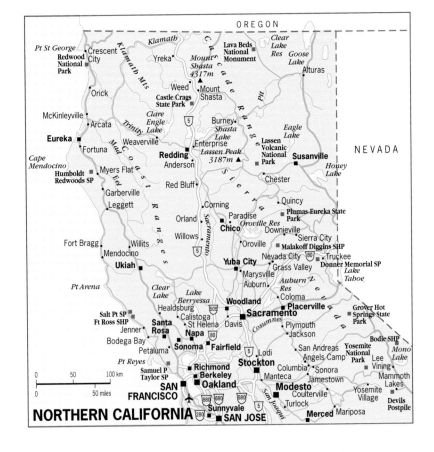

SALES TAX

Remember that sales tax is always added to the marked price in California. Nothing is more frustrating than waiting in a long queue at a cash register to find that the item you thought you just had enough money to buy has an additional 7 per cent to 8.5 per cent added. The exact rate will depend on the town you are in.

WET SUITS REQUIRED

What about the sun and sand? The beaches are not all golden and sun drenched. This is not the state to visit for sunbathing. Certainly the weather can bewarm but the Pacific Ocean is

Gulls and Getty at Malibu – nature and art in harmony

definitely not. You will see plenty of blond, bronzed surfers wherever waves form but the bronzed bodies will be covered in black wet suits to keep out the cold.

Plenty of good sandy beaches can be found but it is the wild, rocky shores for which California is justifiably famous. From Big Sur up to the Oregon border the Pacific waves crash on to some of the most dramatic shoreline you will ever see. Point Lobos near Monterey has been described as the greatest meeting of land and water on earth.

WATER

For all practical purposes the state can be divided into two. Northern California and southern California are as different as chalk and cheese – geographically and politically. The rivalry between the two can be intense and each area has its admirers who will accept no criticism of their chosen land.

The southern half of California is desert. The climate is warm and dry and the insatiable thirst of the giant metropolis of Los Angeles necessitates the diversion of water from the north. The sight of massed lawn sprinklers and gallons of water from washed cars disappearing down the drain is enough to make many northern Californians apoplectic.

For several years water shortage has been a problem throughout California, not just the desert south. Mild winters failed to deliver the snow pack that is needed to provide meltwater to replenish reservoirs. During the most critical periods even restaurants will post notices about only serving water on request, which always seems a bit extreme but indicates the gravity of the situation.

ETHNIC EVOLUTION

The majority of Californians speak English, but California is the ultimate melting-pot of cultures, and each ethnic group has had its impact.

There is a very strong Spanish influence, and the state did in fact start its life as a province of Spanish Mexico. In agricultural areas it is sometimes impossible to find anyone who can understand English. There are towns in the central valley where Spanish is the

Demonstrating their wares in Balboa Park

first and only language.

The recent influx of Asians has already created areas in major cities where Asian languages predominate and even shops signs are in Asian scripts. San Francisco's Chinatown is a classic example, where 40,000 Chinese live in a totally Chinese environment. In Los Angeles a Korean neighbourhood has sprung up in the last few years that is as Korean as areas of Seoul.

California is a state in evolution, a place to test new ideas, a place to live on the cutting edge. It is very difficult to shock the sophisticated Californian.

By any standards California's history is very recent. Any building over 100 years old is of significant importance, and if it is over 150 years old it is as revered as if it were the Tower of London. Where else in the world could you find an archaeological dig on a site dating back to 1917?

The colourful architecture, restaurants and cafés of Horton Plaza in San Diego combine to make shopping a pleasure!

The food at San Francisco's Japan Center is good – not so the buildings

The Venice Canals

This is the only area of Venice's canals that has been preserved. This quiet, residential neighbourhood is a peaceful relief from the frenetic activity of Venice Beach. *Allow 1.5 hours*

From Los Angeles take the Santa Monica Freeway (I-10) west to Venice Boulevard. Follow Venice Boulevard west to the ocean. South Venice Boulevard leads to a car park on the sea front. During the summer this fills very early but there are other car parks in the area.

Walk back from the car park on the right-hand side of the street for three blocks until you pass over a small bridge crossing the Grand Canal. Steps lead down to a footpath that runs along the length of the canal.

Cigarette manufacturer Abbot Kinney had a dream of creating a Venice of America. Sixteen miles of canals were dredged from the Santa Monica Bay swamps in 1905, but the discovery of oil spelled doom. The canals became polluted and by 1929 the city had most of them filled in. This one section of the Grand Canal remains.

Walk along the bank to the far end, past the back gardens of an assortment of cottages. Fortunately the snarling dogs that seem to be

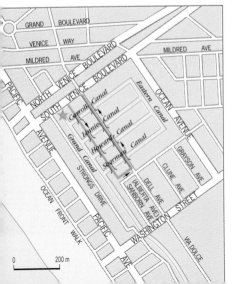

everywhere never materialise and remain safely behind fences. On your left you will pass four canals running at right angles to the Grand Canal. Cross the bridge over the Sherman Canal, the last of the four, and just meander back along the footpaths and enjoy this oasis of tranquility in the heart of Los Angeles.

The houses that back on to the canals are an interesting architectural mix from modest cottages to mini-palazzos. Too expensive for the far-out, Bohemian fringe of Los Angeles, they attract latter-day yuppies with artistic inclinations.

The attraction of this area is obvious as you stroll along the footpaths. Where else in this giant metropolis can you find

One of the few surviving canals in Venice – all that is left of a dream

the quiet, European atmosphere provided by this turn-of-the-century dream.

Dell Avenue cuts through the canal area and this will take you straight back to South Venice Boulevard when you are ready.

Take along some bread to feed the ducks and other waterfowl that have made these canals their home.

The Venice boardwalk has several fast-food vendors. All the way along Ocean Front Walk you will be able to find every kind of junk food known to the human race. The quintessential Venice restaurant is the Sidewalk Café at 1401 Ocean Front Walk (tel: 213 399 5547), about a 10-minute walk north from Venice Boulevard, where breakfast,

lunch and dinner are served. Here you can sit on the boardwalk and enjoy the free entertainment provided by the usual assortment of Venice *habitués* passing to and fro.

Venice reflections

Balboa Park

Close to the centre of San Diego, Balboa Park has a higher concentration of cultural attractions than anywhere in California. Apart from the world-famous zoo there are 14 different museums and an arts and crafts market. *Allow 2 hours, excluding museum visits*

From downtown San Diego take I-5 north to the Pershing Drive exit, and follow the signs to the zoo. Ample parking is available but carefully note where you left your car – the car park is vast!

1 SAN DIEGO ZOO

The world's biggest zoo deserves a day to itself. It first opened as part of the 1915 Panama–California Exposition and became one of the first zoos to take animals out of cages and put them into a natural environment.

The walk starts by the main entrance to the zoo and follows the signs to Balboa Park. After leaving Zoo Place you will pass a 48-seat miniature railroad on your left.

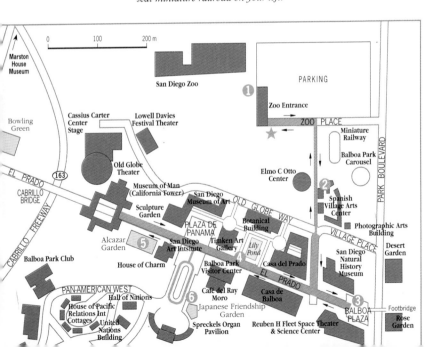

2 SPANISH VILLAGE ART CENTER

Immediately on your left you will see a collection a low, Spanish-style buildings. This arts and crafts complex houses the studios of 42 wood carvers, potters, painters, sculptors, photographers and silversmiths whom you can watch at work and, of course, buy the works they produce. The Center was originally built as part of the 1935–6 California–Pacific Exhibition. (Open: daily 11am–4pm.)

Cross the Village Place and pass between the San Diego Natural History Museum on your left and the Spanish baroque Casa del Prado on your right. Continue to El Prado and turn left.

3 BALBOA PLAZA

This is the end of El Prado. The Inez Grant Parker Memorial Rose Garden will be behind you as you look down El Prado to the landmark California Tower. You can reach the garden across the footbridge over Park Boulevard. It is an All-American Rose Selection Display Garden. Next to the Rose Garden is the Desert Garden with a wide variety of succulents indigenous to the desert.

Walk down El Prado between the ornate Spanish–Mexican-style buildings towards the California Tower.

4 THE LILY POND

During World War II this was used as a swimming pool for patients at the US naval hospital. The steel frame structure behind the pond is the Botanical Building containing over 500 species of tropical and subtropical plants.

Continue down El Prado towards the California Tower. After passing the Timken Art Gallery on your right, El Prado is open to vehicular traffic. Cross the Plaza de Panama and on your left on the corner,

after joining El Prado, is the San Diego Art Institute. Walk along the porticos adjoining it and in an enclosed courtyard to the side is the Alcazar Garden.

5 THE ALCAZAR GARDEN

Designed for the 1915 Panama–California Exposition, it is modelled on the gardens of the Alcázar in Seville, Spain, which were destroyed during the Spanish Civil War. It is an ideal hideaway for a quiet picnic.

Return to the Plaza de Panama and turn right.

6 JAPANESE FRIENDSHIP GARDEN

On your left is a traditional Japanese garden adapted to the climate and topography of San Diego. It provides a perfect place for quiet contemplation. Next to the garden is the Spreckels Organ Pavilion, but unless you are in the park on a Sunday at 2pm, the world's biggest organ will be protected behind a 12-ton metal curtain.

Return to the Plaza de Panama, turn right on to El Prado, and retrace your path back to the zoo.

Balboa Park is the ideal place for a picnic but the Sculpture Garden Café near the Museum of Art Sculpture Garden serves excellent light lunches. (Open: Tuesday to Friday 10am–2.30pm and 5.30pm–8pm; Saturday and Sunday 10am–8pm.)

A more formal and romantic setting can be found in the Café del Rey Moro. This re-creation of a Moorish palace in Spain has a romantically landscaped terrace, indoor dining and a piano bar (open: Mondays, for lunch only; Tuesday to Sunday, lunch and dinner, tel: 619 234 8511).

17-Mile Drive, Pebble Beach

Pebble Beach is an exclusive residential development set amid forests and golf courses by a fabulously beautiful coastline. The 17-Mile Drive was originally named for the horse-drawn carriage ride from the Hotel Del Monte in Monterey out to the Del Monte Forest, though today the drive is much shorter than 17 miles.

The drive can be started at either the southern entrance at the Carmel Gate on Ocean Avenue or in the north at the Pacific Grove Gate on Sunset Drive. It is virtually impossible to get lost as the whole drive is very well signposted.

Pebble Beach is a private estate and a toll is charged for using the road. This is refundable if you eat at the Pebble Beach Lodge. *Allow 1.5 hours*

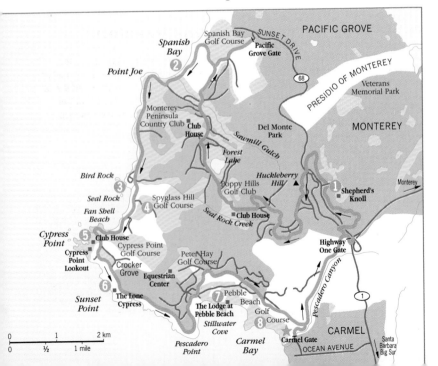

Start at the Carmel Gate and turn right on to the 17-Mile Drive. Follow the signs.

1 SHEPHERD'S KNOLL

This high point on the drive gives spectacular views of Monterey Bay and the San Gablian Mountains.
The road passes through the Del Monte Forest and hillsides covered with huckleberry bushes. Nestled in the woods are the luxurious homes of some of California's wealthiest families.

2 SPANISH BAY AND THE RESTLESS SEA

In 1769, Juan Gaspar de Portolá camped here while trying to locate Monterey Bay; today it is the perfect spot to have a picnic and watch the waves crash. Even on a calm day colliding ocean currents guarantee spectacular waves.
A walking trail along the coastal bluff starts here and continues past some of Monterey Bay's richest tidepools.

3 SEAL AND BIRD ROCKS

These landmark offshore rocks are home to a huge colony of shoreline birds, particularly the double-crested cormorant. There is also a large population of California sea lions and harbour seals that can be heard barking in the distance.

4 SPYGLASS HILL GOLF COURSE

This is one of six golf courses at Pebble Beach and is rated in the top 40 in the US. It is said that Robert Louis Stevenson was inspired by the view from this, his favourite hill, while writing *Treasure Island.* Each of the course's 18 holes takes its name from this classic.
As you drive by, it is not unusual to see deer sharing the golf courses with the golfers.

5 CYPRESS POINT LOOKOUT

The lookout gives one of the finest views of the coastline on 17-Mile Drive. On a clear day you can see as far as Point Sur Lighthouse, 20 miles south.
Immediately below the lookout is a breeding area for harbour seals and in the spring the newborn seal pups can be watched from above.

6 THE LONE CYPRESS

This solitary cypress clinging to an apparently bare rock has become one of California's most familiar landmarks. It is also the symbol of the Pebble Beach Company.

7 THE LODGE AT PEBBLE BEACH

This famous resort, built in 1919, offers de luxe accommodation and restaurants with sweeping views of the ocean.

8 PEBBLE BEACH GOLF COURSE

This is considered by many to be the world's premier golf course. It opened at the same time as the Lodge in 1919 and has become the home of many of the great tournaments of North America.

Cypress Point

Cannery Row and Pacific Grove

Cannery Row was immortalised by John Steinbeck's book of the same name. This walk combines superb coastal scenery with great marine wildlife viewing and passes through some of the most historic sections of Monterey. *Allow 2 hours, excluding a visit to the aquarium.*

Start at the car park for Fisherman's Wharf off Del Monte Avenue.

1 FISHERMAN'S WHARF

This prime sightseeing attraction no longer attracts many fishermen. Commercial fishing is now based on the Municipal Wharf and the original Fisherman's Wharf is little more than a collection of souvenir shops and tourist restaurants. A couple of fish and crab stands still operate but most of the wharf is a highly successful commercial venture and, judging by the crowds, apparently provides just what the tourist wants.

At the end of the wharf an observation deck gives excellent views of the harbour and the bay.
Turn right on to the footpath as soon as you leave Fisherman's Wharf and walk through Fisherman's Shoreline Park to the Coast Guard Wharf.

2 COAST GUARD WHARF

In the winter months take the time to walk out to the end of

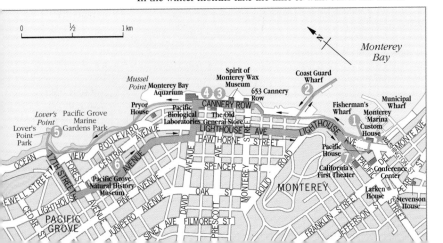

the pier. Every year hundreds of California sea lions congregate here and you can watch them basking in the sun from a few feet away.

Leaving the wharf, turn right on to Cannery Row, and follow it to the end.

3 CANNERY ROW

John Steinbeck knew a very different Cannery Row to the one that now exists. Gone are the stinking fish canneries, to be replaced by attractions such as the Steinbeck's Spirit of Monterey Wax Museum and the Paul Masson Winery Museum. Only Doc Ricketts's Marine Lab at 800 Cannery Row stands relatively unchanged, although it is now a private club.

Kalisa's La Ida Café at the far end of Cannery Row is the only other remnant of the Steinbeck era. The rest is souvenir shops, restaurants and more souvenir shops.

4 MONTEREY BAY AQUARIUM

This state-of-the-art aquarium is devoted exclusively to the marine life of Monterey Bay. Centre-piece of the aquarium is a three-storey-tall giant kelp forest that encapsulates life in the Bay.

There is a 30-foot-deep sea otter tank, numerous tidepool and touching exhibits, and outdoor observation decks.

From the aquarium follow the trail to Lover's Point in Pacific Grove. The trail overlooks the wild, rocky scenery of Monterey Bay.

5 LOVER'S POINT

Pacific Grove is famous for the thousands of monarch butterflies that migrate through here every winter when it becomes 'Butterfly Town, USA'. A butterfly sculpture is prominently displayed in the small park on this

promontory sticking out into the bay.

Take 17th Street for two blocks and turn left on to Lighthouse Avenue.

Steinbeck never saw it so pristine

6 LIGHTHOUSE AVENUE

Seventeenth Street enters Lighthouse Avenue in the middle of Pacific Grove's busy shopping area. This wide street has lots of charm with interesting shops and some fine Victorian architecture.

Continue past a section of residential development to David Avenue where Lighthouse Avenue makes a sudden turn left and then right. Here the character of the avenue changes and the area becomes much more cosmopolitan with a wide range of ethnic restaurants and small shops.

Continue to the Presidio.

7 CALIFORNIA'S FIRST THEATRE

Pass through the Presidio and turn right on to Pacific Street, where you will find the first theatre built in California and still going strong with nightly performances of Victorian melodramas.

Cross Pacific Street through the Custom House Mall and back to the Fisherman's Wharf car park.

Carmel Walk

Carmel-by-the-Sea is the jewel of the central California coast, and this walk through the town and along the beach will show the best that Carmel has to offer. It is located only 2 hours south of San Francisco. *Allow 2 hours*

The best place to start is at the junction of Dolores Street and Ocean Avenue. The popularity of Carmel combined with the limited amount of parking available is a perennial problem. There is a small public car park at the end of Ocean Avenue, but apart from that there are only 2-hour parking meters. Fortunately the town is so small that nowhere is too far.

1 OCEAN AVENUE

This is the main shopping street in Carmel with an enticing collection of boutiques and art galleries. Off Ocean Avenue is a rabbit warren of alleyways and courtyards crammed with even more shops, galleries and restaurants.

Carmel has long been associated with the arts, particularly photography. Just off Ocean Avenue at 6th and Dolores, the Weston Gallery exhibits prints by Ansel Adams and Edward Weston among many other notable photographers. Photography West at Dolores and Ocean has a similarly impressive display of fine photographs.

Walk down Ocean Avenue towards the ocean. At the car parking area walk on to the beach and turn left.

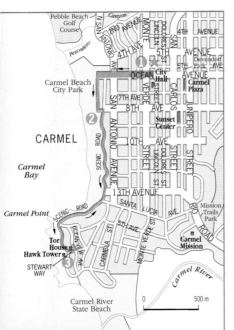

2 THE BEACH

The best way to experience this walk to the full is to throw off your shoes and socks and get the sand between your toes. Even in December and January the weather can be sunny and warm, and this is one of the best stretches of sand on the coast. The beach sweeps around to the rocks at the southern tip of Carmel Bay.

You do not have to walk on the sand. Scenic Road runs parallel to the

Tor House, built by Robinson Jeffers from boulders hauled up from the beach

beach and it was not named accidentally. It gives unequalled views of the coast.

However, it is better to start on the beach as the first section of Scenic Road does not have a footpath and cars can come perilously close on this narrow street. Scenic Road can be reached from the beach at several points by easily spotted wooden steps.

The sandy beach ends at a group of surf-spattered rocks at the southern end. It is possible to scramble over these rocks but it is far safer to climb up the last wooden steps to the footpath by Scenic Road if you have not already done so. *Continue south on the footpath.*

3 TOR HOUSE

After a short distance you will see a house jutting out spectacularly over the sea. Look left and there you will see a medieval-looking stone tower and a rambling house constructed from huge boulders. This was the was the home of the great American poet, Robinson Jeffers.

To get to the house turn left up Stewart Way and then left again on to Ocean View Avenue. Tor House is two houses down on the left.

Jeffers built the house and tower with his own hands, hauling the granite stones by horse from the little cove below. The house was modelled after an English Tudor barn, and took him less than four years to complete. Jeffers built it using a block and tackle system and wooden planks, similar to methods used by the ancient Egyptians. He lived here from 1919 until his death in 1962. One wing of the house is still occupied by his daughter-in-law, Lee. Hawk Tower was built as a retreat for his wife.

Tor House is open for tours on Fridays and Saturdays between 10am and 4pm, strictly by appointment. For reservations tel: 408 624 1813 or write to The Tor House Foundation, Box 1887, Carmel, California 93921
Return to Ocean Avenue by the same route.

49-Mile Drive

If you only have one day to see San Francisco then take this drive. It passes virtually every major sight in San Francisco. *Allow 4 hours*

Where you start is not important, though it is better to plan the drive so that you avoid the congested downtown area during rush hours. The route is well marked with '49-Mile Drive' blue-and-white seagull signs, so it is difficult to get lost.
From Union Square take Post Street to Grant Avenue, turn left and drive through the Chinatown Gate to California Street.

1 CHINATOWN
The junction of California and Grant is the heart of Chinatown.

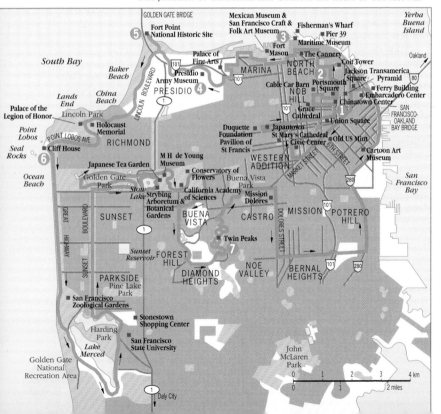

Cable cars run along this section of California Street – remember that they always have right of way.
Continue up to Nob Hill, pass between the Mark Hopkin's Hotel on the left and the Fairmont on the right. Continue past the Flood Mansion and turn right in front of Grace Cathedral on to Taylor Street.

Turn right on to Washington Street and the Cable Car Barn is on the left at the junction with Mason Street. Follow the signs as far as Kearny Street.

2 PORTSMOUTH SQUARE

A lift from the car park goes straight into Portsmouth Square. This is the social centre of Chinatown.
Turn left on to Kearny, follow the signs through North Beach as far as Lombard Street, and turn left. Coit Tower is a short detour to the right.

Follow the signs, pass Pier 39 and drive along Fisherman's Wharf to Ghiradelli Square. Take Bay Street to Marina Boulevard.

3 FORT MASON

This collection of old warehouses and wharves is now home to over 50 non-profit organisations, including Greenpeace, and three small museums: the Mexican Museum, the Museo Italio–Americano and the San Francisco Craft and Folk Art Museum. The SS *Jeremiah O'Brien* is also moored here.
Follow the signs through the Marina District, pass the Palace of Fine Arts and enter the Presidio on Lincoln Boulevard.

4 THE PRESIDIO

Established by the Spanish in 1776 and taken over by the United States in 1846, these 1,440 acres of wooded hills are an army base. The drive passes the Presidio Army Museum, protected by antique cannon and housing a collection of military uniforms and weapons.
Continue on Lincoln Boulevard and turn off at Long Avenue.

5 FORT POINT

At the end of the road nestling under the girders of the Golden Gate Bridge is Fort Point, the only brick fort to be built west of the Mississippi.
Return to Lincoln Boulevard and continue to the end. In Lincoln Park pass the California Palace of the Legion of Honor and turn right on Point Lobos Avenue.

6 CLIFF HOUSE

This far western point of San Francisco juts out into the Pacific. The Cliff House has restaurants, shops and great views of Seal Rock with its colony of sea lions. Below the Cliff House the Musée Méchanique has a fascinating collection of working arcade machines.
The road passes the wide expanse of Ocean Beach and hugs the coast until it passes the Zoo on the left, and continues around Lake Merced where it turns north and follows Sunset Boulevard to Golden Gate Park. Follow the signs on the meandering route through the park and climb up to the summit of Twin Peaks.

7 TWIN PEAKS

The 910-foot summit offers a 360-degree panorama of San Francisco.
Continue down across Market Street to Dolores Street. Pass Mission Dolores on the right and continue through the Mission District to Potrero Hill. Take Highway 280 north to the 6th Street exit. Follow Howard Street to the Embarcadero Center and follow the signs through the Financial District down Market Street to the Civic Center, on to Japantown and return to Union Square down Post Street.

CALIFORNIA

NEVADA

• Mendocino

• Napa

• San Francisco

San Francisco Waterfront

This walk combines some of the best views of the Bay with several major tourist sites, good shopping, street entertainment and great food. *Allow 1.5 hours*

Start from the Pier 39 multi-storey car park between the Embarcadero and North Point. There is usually space available here and with validation with a purchase from one of Pier 39's shops or restaurants the parking fee is quite reasonable.

1 PIER 39

This old steamship wharf is now a two-level shopping and restaurant complex. The street performers here provide some of the best free entertainment in town, and the views from the end of the pier are some of the best of the bay. Between September and May, hundreds of California sea lions can be seen from the viewing area at K Dock.
From Pier 39 continue west along the Embarcadero keeping as close to the waterfront as possible.

2 USS *PAMPANITO*

This restored World War II fleet submarine, a veteran of six Pacific patrols, sits at Pier 45. Tours are given daily (tel: 415 929 0202). Open: Sunday to Thursday 9am–6pm; Friday and Saturday 9am–9pm. Admission charge.

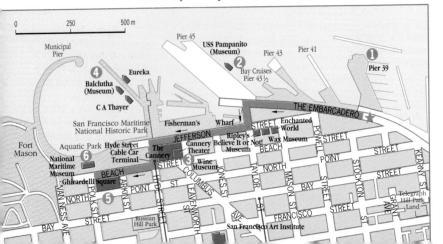

To avoid the main tourist traffic and to experience the old flavour of Fisherman's Wharf, continue along the waterfront by Pier 45 which still has a small working fishing fleet.

Return to Jefferson Street and continue along to the Cannery on the left-hand side of the street.

3 THE CANNERY

This multi-storied shopping complex was once a fruit and vegetable canning factory for the Del Monte Corporation. During the summer, street performers entertain shoppers in the pleasant central courtyard.

From shipping to shopping

Continue along Jefferson Street to Hyde Street.

4 HYDE STREET PIER

On the right-hand side of the street as it opens out into Aquatic Park is Hyde Street Pier, which is part of the National Maritime Museum. Several historic ships are anchored here including the *Eureka,* an 1890 ferryboat; the *Balclutha,* a Scottish merchant ship built in 1886 that rounded Cape Horn no less than 17 times carrying coal, wine and hardware from Europe; and a three-masted schooner, *C A Thayer,* that carried timber down the California coast.

San Francisco Maritime National Historical Park

2905 Hyde Street, San Francisco (tel: 415 556 6435)

Open: daily 9.30am–5.30pm (until 4.30pm in the winter)

Admission charge

Walk up Hyde Street past the cable car turntable at the junction with Beach Street. Turn right on to Beach and continue past the street vendors selling arts and crafts. There are good views out over Aquatic Park. Continue to Larkin Street.

5 GHIRARDELLI SQUARE

At the junction of Larkin and Beach is one of San Francisco's most attractive shopping and restaurant developments. Ghirardelli Square was originally the home of Ghirardelli chocolate which is still highly regarded in the US. You can see the antique chocolate machines working and even sample the goods (see Shopping).

Ghirardelli Square

900 North Point Street, San Francisco (tel: 415 775 5500)

Return to Beach Street and turn left.

6 THE NATIONAL MARITIME MUSEUM

Opposite Ghirardelli Square, the National Maritime Museum has a display of model ships, photographs and various nautical memorabilia.

National Maritime Museum

Beach and Polk Streets, San Francisco (tel: 415 556 2904)

Open: daily 10am–5pm

Admission free

Return the same way to Pier 39 or take the cable car from the Hyde Street terminal.

CALIFORNIA
NEVADA
• Mendocino
• Napa
• San Francisco

Downtown San Francisco

San Francisco is one of the few American cities that lends itself to walking. This walk covers the best areas of the commercial, shopping and historic areas of downtown San Francisco. *Allow 2 hours*

Start from Union Square. On the Stockton Street side of the Square look for Maiden Lane. This narrow street has exclusive boutiques and galleries. On the left you will see a Frank Lloyd Wright building that was a model for New York's Guggenheim Museum. Follow Maiden Lane to Kearny Street, turn left, walk to Post Street and turn right.

1 CROCKER GALLERIA
This glass-domed shopping mall off Montgomery Street was modelled on the Galleria in Milan.
Continue along the canyon of Montgomery Street, the Wall Street of the West. This is the financial heart of northern California.

2 TRANSAMERICA PYRAMID
The unmistakable building on the corner of Montgomery and Washington streets is the tallest structure in the city at 853 feet. The 27th floor has a viewing area open to the public on weekdays.
Continue along Montgomery Street. Once out of the financial area, the street starts to climb. Continue up the increasingly steep street as far as Vallejo Street. There are good views of both the city and the bay.

Turn right and descend to Battery Street. Turn left. This is the centre of the advertising industry and all the major agencies are along here. Continue along Battery to Levi Plaza, the home of Levi Strauss. Opposite is Filbert Street.

The metronome-like TransAm Pyramid

3 FILBERT STREET STEPS

The steps rise steeply from Battery Street straight up to Coit Tower. The steps are one of the undiscovered treasures of the city. They pass carefully tended gardens and a profusion of flowers during the summer months.

4 COIT TOWER

The steps emerge at this distinctive landmark on top of Telegraph Hill. Inside the tower there are wonderful murals painted during the 1930s depicting the workers of San Francisco. The top of the tower gives good views of the city and the bay.
From the tower continue down Filbert Street to the Italian North Beach District. Walk as far as Stockton Street and turn left. The coffee and garlic aromas of North Beach will give way to smells of Chinatown.

5 STOCKTON STREET

Always busy, Stockton Street is where the Chinese shop. This is the real Chinatown.
Continue along Stockton to Washington Street. Turn left and walk one block to Grant Avenue. Turn right. Grant is the tourists' Chinatown with gift shops, jewellers and restaurants.

6 CHINATOWN GATEWAY

Chinatown ends at this imposing gate guarded by a pair of dragons.
Turn right on to Sutter Street. Here are some of the most fashionable and expensive shops in San Francisco. Walk up Sutter to Powell Street. Turn left on Powell and return to Union Square.

Cable cars and steeply sloping streets epitomise San Francisco

Silverado Trail

This country drive not only avoids the heavy traffic of Highway 29 through Napa Valley but passes through some of the most scenic, and unspoiled, sections of the California wine country. The Silverado Trail was originally a stagecoach route and even today it has a strong feeling of the past. *Allow 2 hours, including stops*

Travelling north, turn right off Highway 29 at Trancas Street in Napa. Follow Trancas for one mile and turn left on to the Silverado Trail.

Half a mile along the Silverado Trail turn right on to Hardman Avenue. At the end of Hardman turn right and the Silverado Country Club is on the left.

1 SILVERADO COUNTRY CLUB

This magnificent plantation-style building was originally the 1870 home of General John Miller. It is now one of the finest resort facilities in California with two championship golf courses, 20 tennis courts and two gourmet restaurants.
Return to the Silverado Trail and turn right. Drive for two miles passing rolling vineyards on both sides of the road.

2 STAG'S LEAP WINE CELLARS

This is the winery that put Napa Valley on the international wine map in the 1970s when one of its Cabernet Sauvignon wines beat the best French wines at a blind tasting in Paris.

The winery has a tasting room open to the public, and tours are available by appointment.
5766 Silverado Trail, Napa (tel: 707 944 2020)
Continue north on the Silverado Trail passing several small wineries. Turn left on to Oakville Cross Road. Enter the first drive on the right.

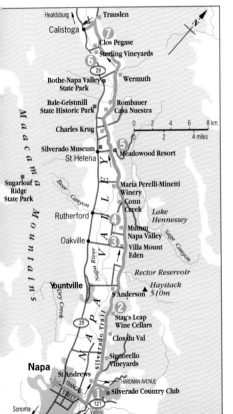

3 VILLA MOUNT EDEN
This small winery, built in 1881 and encircled by an 87-acre vineyard, is one of the few examples of the original Napa wineries. It is open for both tours and tasting.
620 Oakville Cross Road, Oakville (tel: 707 944 2414)
Continue north along the Silverado Trail for about one mile. Mumm Napa Valley is on the left.

4 MUMM NAPA VALLEY
In complete contrast to Villa Mount Eden, this state-of-the-art winery, owned in part by the great French champagne house, is one of the few producers of champagne-style wines in the valley. Open for both tours and tasting.
8445 Silverado Trail, Rutherford (tel: 707 942 3300)
Drive two miles north to Howell Mountain Road. Turn right and then immediately left on to a winding lane.

5 MEADOWOOD RESORT
Beautifully situated in the midst of a tree-covered valley, the Meadowood

Not an English country house, but Meadowood Resort in Napa Valley

Resort provides a secluded retreat with golf, tennis, fine dining and a perfectly manicured croquet lawn.
900 Meadowood Lane, St Helena (tel: 800 458 8080)
The Trail winds north through yet more vineyards. After four miles, turn left on to Dunaweal Lane.

6 STERLING VINEYARDS
An aerial tram transports visitors to this hilltop winery for magnificent views down the Napa Valley.
1111 Dunaweal Lane, Calistoga (tel: 707 942 5151)

7 CLOS PEGASE
Directly across the road from Sterling, the controversial architecture of this winery is hard to miss. Inside you will find a very impressive art collection.
1060 Dunaweal Lane, Calistoga (tel: 707 942 4981.
Continue along the Silverado Trail to its end in Calistoga. Turn left into town.

CALIFORNIA
NEVADA

• Mendocino

• Napa

• San Francisco

Mendocino Headlands

This windswept town on the often fog-shrouded bluffs overlooking the Pacific could easily be mistaken for New England rather than California. In fact, film-makers have been using Mendocino as a New England look-alike since *Johnny Belinda* was made there almost 50 years ago.

Walking is the only way to see Mendocino and this walk explores not only the historic buildings and film trivia but also the wild and rugged coast and beaches of the Mendocino Headlands. *Allow 2 hours*

Driving north on Highway 1, turn off at the first Mendocino exit on to Main Street. The walk starts at the Presbyterian Church on the left-hand side of the road.

1 MENDOCINO PRESBYTERIAN CHURCH
This is the oldest Presbyterian Church in continuous operation in California. In 1947 it was the set for *Johnny Belinda* starring Jane Wyman.
Continue along Main Street, past Lansing Street to Kelly House set back from the street on the right-hand side.

2 KELLY HOUSE MUSEUM
Built in 1861, Kelly House is now a Victorian museum and houses the Mendocino Historical Research Library. The town's public toilets are across the road on Main Street.

Nearby

The Café Beaujolais, at the junction of Ukiah and Evergreen Streets, is one of the most highly acclaimed restaurants in California. Their breakfasts are outstanding, and they are also open for lunch and dinner (tel: 707 937 5614).

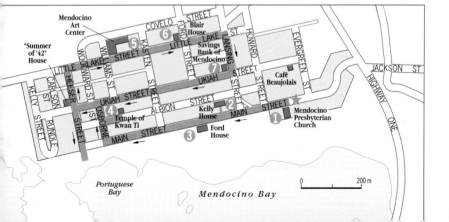

East Coast buildings on the West Coast

Cross Main Street and turn right. Ford House is on the left.

3 FORD HOUSE

Also a museum, Ford House was built in 1854 and houses the town's Visitor Information Bureau. There is an excellent large-scale model showing Mendocino as it was early this century. Many of the original wooden buildings of Mendocino have been destroyed by fire, and this is one of the oldest still standing. *Cross Main Street again and walk past the boutiques and galleries to Osborne Street. Turn right and right again on to Albion Street.*

4 THE TEMPLE OF KWAN TI

This small, red building houses an old Chinese temple which can be visited by appointment only (tel: 707 937 4506). *Return to Osborne Street, turn right, walk to Ukiah Street, turn left and continue to Heeser Street. The old house on the right corner of Heeser and Ukiah was the set for the film 'The Summer of '42'. Turn right on to Heeser and walk up to Little Lake Street. Turn right and continue to Williams Street.*

5 MENDOCINO ART CENTER

The Art Center has achieved a national reputation and a small gallery has exhibits of both local and national artists. *Continue along Little Lake Street to Ford Street.*

6 BLAIR HOUSE

Mendocino is full of charming bed-and-breakfast inns, and Blair House has the added attraction that it was the location for the television series *Murder, She Wrote*, starring Angela Lansbury. *Continue to Lansing Street and turn right. Stay on the right-hand side of the street and walk to the corner of Ukiah Street.*

7 SAVINGS BANK OF MENDOCINO

This architectural landmark is topped by a superb redwood sculpture of Father Time. The building was originally the Masonic Temple. *Turn right on to Ukiah and walk to Heeser Street. Turn left, go to Main Street, and take the trail to the headlands. Steps lead down from the bluff to Portuguese Beach.*

The Bluffs at Mendocino

What to See – Los Angeles

*I*n LA, as everyone calls it, the car is king. The city is so large that walking is totally impractical, while public transport is rudimentary at best. Fortunately for the visitor, hiring a car is both simple and cheap, as long as you are 25 or over and hold a valid driving licence.

A few millimetres on a map can take hours to drive, a problem that is caused as much by traffic as by distance. But the distances are impressive. The size of Los Angeles is difficult to comprehend until you try to drive from one neighbourhood to another on one of the urban freeways.

From the visitor's perspective, it is impossible to tell where LA begins or ends. Los Angeles County has a population of almost 9 million and covers an area of 4,083 square miles with 88 incorporated cities, and the continuous urban sprawl goes way beyond this.

Development stretches from Ventura County in the north to Orange County and Long Beach in the south, and from the Pacific coast across to Riverside County in the east.

This five-county area is bigger than any state excluding California, New York and Texas and houses 14.5 million people in 34,149 square miles.

Driving at the speed limit, it takes over 2 hours to cross the conurbation. However, being able to travel at anything approaching the speed limit is

Downtown Los Angeles architecture

considered a minor miracle. During rush hours there is so much traffic that even the most modest journey can take in excess of 2 hours.

You could easily spend three weeks in LA and still not have time to do and see everything.

Los Angeles has it all – except for clean air. On rare days during the winter Santa Ana winds blow away the smog to reveal the San Bernardino mountains forming a spectacular backdrop to the city. On days like this it really becomes the city of angels.

Los Angeles has had much negative media coverage in the last few years, particularly relating to street violence. Although there are probably more problems here than any other part of California, as one might expect for such a large city, the areas to which visitors are likely to travel are as safe as most cities of the world. Guard against pickpockets and do not leave valuables unprotected and most problems will be avoided.

The pockets of potential violence are usually far away from the tourist sites. Not visiting Disneyland because of gang wars in Watts is like avoiding Paris because of civil war in Yugoslavia.

BEVERLY HILLS

For the mere mortal Beverly Hills is a place to ogle. This super-exclusive independent township surrounded by Los Angeles was originally bean fields but soon became the preferred address for Hollywood celebrities.

Elegant mansions can be glimpsed hiding behind security fences and you may even spot the occasional film star, although many of the houses are more likely to be occupied by doctors, lawyers or oil barons.

How the other half live – Beverly Hills

Douglas Fairbanks and Mary Pickford built Pickfair at 1143 Summit Drive and it became a focal point for the Hollywood set. Mary Pickford lived there in complete seclusion until her death in 1980.

The homes of the stars can be found either with the aid of maps on sale at many street corners or more reliably on a bus tour through the town.

A more intimate brush with Hollywood can be had at the sumptuous Beverly Hills Hotel, which was built in 1912. The hotel's legendary Polo Lounge has been, and continues to be, the setting for many a Hollywood deal. If you want to be in films, this is the place to be seen.

Apart from the shopping areas around Rodeo Drive (see **Shopping**) there are few footpaths in Beverly Hills and walking is frowned upon.

Expect to be questioned by the police if you get out of your Ferrari or Mercedes and they find you wandering aimlessly about.

BUENA PARK
Orange County

This nondescript town off I-5, a few minutes drive from Anaheim, used to have several attractions for the visitor. Business has fallen recently, however, and most of these attractions have closed down, though two remain that perfectly complement a visit to Disneyland.

Knott's Berry Farm
Although this was originally exactly what its name implies, Walter Knott started to add attractions to the farm in the 1920s. It is now California's second biggest tourist enticement with over 165 rides and attractions covering over 150 acres.

The emphasis of the theme park is on America's past. There is a ghost town, a 19th-century train running around the grounds, a Roaring Twenties area with thrill rides and a penny arcade and Bigfoot Rapids – a very wet ride down California's longest man-made white-water river. If you need even more thrills, Montezooma's Revenge will propel you to 55mph in 5 seconds both upside down and backwards!

The perfect antidote to all this excitement is the spectacular display of water jets and fountains choreographed to classical music.
8039 Beach Boulevard, (tel: 714 220 5200). Open: Sunday to Friday, 9am–midnight; Saturday, 9am–1am Admission charge

Movieland Wax Museum
Over 200 life-size wax models of film and televison stars, from Laurel and Hardy to Rambo and Startrek, inhabit authentic-looking sets. A collection of Hollywood memorabilia completes the exhibit.

If you like exhibits of wax figures, this one is very well done.

Tradition and the twentieth century mingle here in LA's Chinatown

7711 Beach Boulevard, Buena Park (tel: 714 522 1154). Open: Sunday to Thursday 9am–11pm; Friday and Saturday 10am–10pm. Admission charge

CHINATOWN

Compared wth San Francisco, LA's Chinatown is tiny. It is easily seen on foot and consists of the usual array of Chinese restaurants, Chinese groceries and shops selling cheap novelties imported from the Far East.

North Spring Street and North Broadway form the two main thoroughfares and the Kong Chow Temple on the second floor of 931 North Broadway is well worth a visit (tel: 213 626 1955).

CITY HALL

Downtown Los Angeles is a major business centre with little of interest for the non-business visitor. However, City Hall is architecturally interesting, being the first high-rise building to be constructed in the city.

The observation deck on the 27th floor gives excellent views of the city (smog permitting!).

In the entrance hall is a holographic portrait of Mayor Tom Bradley.
200 North Spring Street, Los Angeles (tel: 213 485 2121). Open: Monday to Friday, 9am–4pm. Admission free

DISNEYLAND

California's number one tourist attraction includes 7 'theme' lands extending over 80 acres, while an additional 102 acres provides parking for 15,167 vehicles!

The Lands are:
Adventureland – exotic regions of Asia, Africa and the South Pacific

Knott's Berry Farm at Anaheim

Critterland – backwoods setting for Splash Mountain
Fantasyland – fairytale kingdom
Frontierland – the world of the pioneers of the Old West
Main Street USA – smalltown America at the turn of the century
New Orleans Square – home of pirates, ghosts and quaint shops
Tomorrowland – the world of the future.

A full day is certainly not enough to do justice to Disneyland. Get there early and list priorities with the aid of the map and brochure given at the entrance.

Disneyland is open every day of the year with extended hours during the summer months. Weekends during the summer are the busiest time when over 9,000 staff are employed! There are always crowds of visitors but queues at the attractions are generally shorter at the beginning of the week.
Location: 27 miles southeast of Los Angeles Civic Center in Anaheim. To verify Park hours, tel: 714 999 4565

EXPOSITION PARK

This 114-acre park close to downtown LA is the home of the 92,000-seat Los Angeles Memorial Coliseum that was the site of both the 1932 and 1984 Olympic Games. It is also home to three of the city's major museums.

California Museum of Science and Industry

The museum extends through several buildings with exhibits covering subjects as diverse as AIDS and earthquakes. This is very much a hands-on museum and most of the exhibits are interactive.

Next door is the Aerospace Complex, which not only houses a collection of aircraft and spacecraft, but also an IMAX theatre screening the latest spectacles in 70mm surround vision. *Figueroa Street at Exposition Boulevard (tel: 213 744 7400). Open: daily 10am–5pm. Admission free, but charge for Imax Theatre*

The California Afro-American Museum

This museum is devoted to black culture and history. It is housed in an airy glass building next to the Aerospace Complex and has new exhibits every few months. *Figueroa Street at Exposition Boulevard (tel: 213 744 7432). Open: daily 10am–5pm. Admission charge*

Los Angeles County Museum of Natural History

At the northern end of the park, this is reputedly the most popular museum in Los Angeles. Behind an unimpressive exterior, the Los Angeles County Museum of Natural History houses three floors of galleries which display everything from dioramas of North American and African wildlife to dinosaurs and fossils to cultural exhibits depicting life on the frontier.

There is a particularly good mineral and crystal gallery with a well-guarded room devoted to precious stones. *Tel: 213 744 3414. Open: Tuesday to Sunday, 10am–5pm. Admission charge (but free on 1st Tuesday of each month)*

FARMERS' MARKET

It is doubtful if any farmers actually make it to the market these days, but you will find a wide variety of produce stalls as well as every other type of shop imaginable.

The biggest attractions are numerous snack bars and cafés serving a huge variety of foods, all at affordable prices. *6333 West Third Street, Los Angeles (tel: 213 933 9211). Open: Monday to Saturday, 9am–6.30pm; Sunday, 10am–5pm*

FOREST LAWN

Cemeteries may not be a normal tourist attraction, but Forest Lawn on South Glendale Avenue, close to Griffith Park, is said to have in excess of 1 million visitors a year. There you will be able to find the final resting places of stars such as Clark Gable and Jean Harlow.

This perfectly manicured park is also home to larger-than-life-sized reproductions of some of the world's great masterpieces including Michelangelo's *David* and Leonardo da Vinci's *Last Supper* in stained glass.

You can also see the world's largest religious painting on canvas, Jan Styka's *The Crucifixion*.

The 300 acres of lush lawns are a popular, if macabre, picnic site. *1712 South Glendale Avenue, Glendale (tel: 818 241 4151). Open: daily, 9am–5pm. Admission free*

GRIFFITH PARK

This 4,000-acre oasis of greenery sits astride the Hollywood Hills. It provides outdoor recreational facilities for the neighbourhood, including an 18-hole golf course, more than 53 miles of jogging, hiking and bridle trails and pony rides for youngsters. It is also the home for several important attractions.
Park Ranger Visitor Center, 4730 Crystal Springs Drive, Los Angeles (tel: 213 665 5188)

Gene Autry Western Heritage Museum

On the northeastern edge of the park, this impressive museum dedicated to the 'Wild West' was opened at the end of 1988. Anyone with even the slightest interest in cowboys will be fascinated by the two floors of exhibits of historic artefacts and Western film memorabilia such as the jacket worn by Robert Redford as the Sundance Kid or John Wayne's gun belt. Film clips from old Westerns can be seen on monitors throughout the museum.
4700 Western Heritage Way, Los Angeles (tel: 213 667 2000). Open: Tuesday to Sunday, 10am–5pm. Admission charge

Griffith Observatory and Planetarium

Although it is doubtful if the telescopes could now penetrate more than a few feet of Los Angeles smog, the observatory is still the major landmark of Griffith Park. On a clear day the views of Hollywood and downtown Los Angeles are spectacular.

The 1930s architecture has provided the backdrop for several Hollywood films, most notably for James Dean in *Rebel Without A Cause*.

The Hall of Sciences has displays on astronomy and meteorology, a planetarium, and a laserium presenting the latest in hi-tech light shows.
2800 East Observatory Road, Los Angeles (tel: 213 664 1191). Open: Tuesday to Friday, 2pm–10pm; weekends, 12.30pm–10pm. Admission free (excepting the laserium)

Los Angeles Zoo

The zoo is situated directly opposite the Gene Autry Western Heritage Museum. The 113 acres opened in 1966 and now houses over 2,000 different animals. There is a particularly strong collection of primates and endangered species.
5333 Zoo Drive, Los Angeles (tel: 213 666 4090). Open: daily, 10am–5pm. Admission charge

Travel Town

Close to the zoo, this transportation museum has a yard full of steam engines and rolling stock as well as examples of just about any other form of transport you can think of. There is a narrow-gauge railway on which children can ride.
4730 Crystal Springs Drive, Los Angeles (tel: 213 662 5874). Open: Monday to Friday, 10am–4pm; weekends 10am–5pm. Admission free

Screen cowboys – the Gene Autry Museum

Paramount Studios

Early special effects used in
filming King Kong

The make-up
department at Universal Studios

Hollywood Boulevard

The Movies

Legend has it that in 1913, when a downpour of rain greeted Cecil B DeMille in Arizona, he boarded a train and travelled west until he found sunshine. When he did, Hollywood was born.

It all started in an old barn which now houses the **Hollywood Studio Museum** at *2100 North Highland Avenue (tel: 213 874 2276)*. The museum is full of memorabilia from the silent movies, including a re-creation of DeMille's office.

Today most of the great studios make more films for television than for the cinema, and many of them offer tours.

In Hollywood, **Paramount Studios** at *5555 Melrose Avenue (tel: 213 468 5575)* offer a 2-hour tour with a historical overview.

KCET, a Los Angeles public television station, gives technical tours of its studios at *4401 Sunset Boulevard (tel: 213 666 6500)*.

Burbank Studios at *4000 Warner Boulevard, Burbank (tel: 818 954 1744)*, take you behind the scenes to see the daily activities of both **Columbia Pictures** and **Warner Brothers**. Only small groups are accepted, but a thorough introduction to the whole process of film-making is given.

Of course, the grandaddy of studio tours is at **Universal Studios**, *100 Universal City Plaza, Universal City (tel: 818 508 9600)*. Although this is the Hollywood version of Hollywood it is good entertainment value, if not too authentic in other departments.

To feel a part of the scene you may want to pick up a copy of the *Hollywood Reporter* that has covered 'The Industry' every weekday morning since 1931.

If you really want to get in on the action, the *Motion Picture Coordination Office, 6922 Hollywood Boulevard (tel: 213 485 5324)*, issues a daily shoot sheet giving location details of all films being shot that day.

Hollywood on Location, 8466 Wilshire Boulevard, Beverly Hills (tel: 213 666 6500), offers a more complete service. Every morning they issue a list of every film and television show being filmed around town. Visitors are supplied with a list of locations, maps, titles and the names of stars they are likely to see. There is a substantial charge for the service.

HOLLYWOOD

The area was established as a religious agricultural community in 1903 only to become part of Los Angeles in 1910.

The intersection of Hollywood and Vine has become synonymous with the glitter and glamour of Hollywood. What a contrast the reality is. This depressingly run-down area is one of the seedier districts of Los Angeles.

Hollywood Boulevard is a must-see area, but the sooner out of it the better. The stars set into the pavement – the so-called Walk of Fame – shine through litter and discarded bottles. What a dubious honour having your name set in such undignified surroundings.

Grauman's Chinese Theatre

Built by Sid Grauman in 1927, this cinema is one of the essential sights of Hollywood, not so much for the gaudy false Chinese architecture as for the remarkable collection of autographs in cement in front of the theatre. Not only the autographs but also hand and footprints of film stars such as Cary Grant, Rock Hudson, Doris Day and Joan Crawford. The interior of the theatre is worth a look, with décor equalling the extravagance of the colourful exterior.

6925 Hollywood Boulevard, Hollywood (tel: 213 461 3331). Open: daily, noon–midnight. Admission charge for cinema

Paramount Studios

Most of the major studios have left Hollywood for the San Fernando Valley, and Paramount Studios is the last of the greats to still occupy their lot on Melrose Avenue. Only recently have members of the public been allowed through their famous gateway, and now behind-the-scenes tours are available.

5555 Melrose Avenue, Hollywood (tel: 213 468 5575).
Open: weekdays 8am–4pm.
Admission charge, reservations essential

Hollywood Memorial Park Cemetery

Many of the old Paramount stars are buried here. Among the palm trees and marble statues lie Rudolf Valentino, Peter Finch, Cecil B DeMille, Douglas Fairbanks and many more great Hollywood personalities.

6000 Santa Monica Boulevard.

LA BREA TAR PITS

These bubbling pits of black goop sit incongruously next to the sleek modern architecture of the LA County Museum of Art on Wilshire Boulevard.

During the Pleistocene period over 200 different types of creature were trapped in this primordial ooze, and their perfectly preserved skeletons are still being discovered by paleontologists in one of the richest fossil deposits ever to have been found.

In the adjoining George C Page Museum you can see displays of many of the discoveries from the Ice Age, including skeletons of mastodons, mammoths and ancient horses. You can also see a working paleontology laboratory.

5801 Wilshire Boulevard, Los Angeles (tel: 213 936 2230). Open: Tuesday to Sunday 10am–5pm. Admission charge (but free on 2nd Tuesday of each month)

LITTLE TOKYO

This enclave of Japanese culture is close to City Hall. There are theatres, Buddhist temples and the two-block Japanese Village Plaza, an outdoor shopping and dining mall.

South San Pedro Street, Los Angeles.

LONG BEACH

Long Beach is so far from central Los Angeles that it is difficult to think of it as part of the same county. It has undergone a facelift in recent years and provides a pleasant break from the big city.

Queen Mary Hotel

The world's once biggest ocean liner lies berthed in the world's largest natural harbour. The refurbished *Queen Mary* was retired to Long Beach where it opened as a hotel, museum and entertainment complex. Daily tours of the ship, including the engine rooms, are offered to the public, free to hotel guests. *Pier J, Long Beach (tel: 310 435 3511).*

Little Italy

The neighbourhood of Naples was developed early this century based on the canal towns of Italy. Quiet waterways are linked by a series of walkways and what more appropriate way of seeing the area could there be than by gondola. *Gondola Getaway, 5437 East Ocean Boulevard, Long Beach (tel: 310 433 9595).*

Queen Mary, flanked by the Catalina ferry and the geodesic dome

LOS ANGELES COUNTY MUSEUM OF ART

This is the largest museum in the West and its exhibits cover the history of art from pre-Columbian gold ornaments to late 20th-century paintings. It is a museum of truly international importance, occupying four main buildings around a central courtyard. The recently added Pavilion for Japanese Art houses the Shin'enkan collection of Japanese paintings and *objets d'art.*

The Ahmanson Building houses an outstanding collection of Indian and Buddhist art, along with collections from Africa, the South Seas, Egypt and some of the great masterpieces of the Renaissance, and houses more great art than many major museums.

This is an awe-inspiring collection worthy of hours, if not days, of browsing. *5905 Wilshire Boulevard, Los Angeles (tel: 213 937 2590). Open: Tuesday to Friday, 10am–5pm; weekends 10am–6pm. Admission charge.*

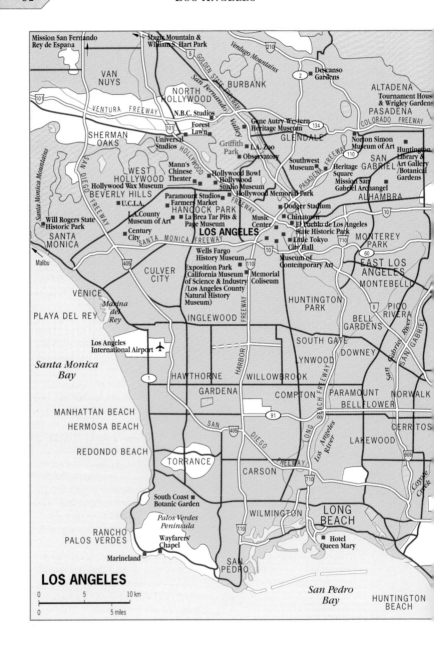

Mission San Fernando
Rey de Espana

Magic Mountain &
William S. Hart Park

VAN
NUYS

BURBANK

NORTH
HOLLYWOOD

Descanso
Gardens

ALTADENA
Tournament House
& Wrigley Gardens

PASADENA
COLORADO FREEWAY

VENTURA FREEWAY

N.B.C. Studios

Forest
Lawn

SHERMAN
OAKS

Gene Autry Western
Heritage Museum

Universal
Studios

Griffith
Park

GLENDALE

L.A. Zoo
Observatory

Norton Simon
Museum of Art

Huntington
Library &
Art Gallery
/Botanical
Gardens

WEST
HOLLYWOOD

Mann's
Chinese
Theater

Hollywood Wax Museum

BEVERLY HILLS

U.C.L.A.

Paramount Studios
Farmers Market

Hollywood Bowl
Hollywood
Studio Museum

Hollywood Memorial Park

Southwest
Museum

SAN
GABRIEL

Heritage
Square
Mission San
Gabriel Archangel

ALHAMBRA

Will Rogers State
Historic Park

HANCOCK PARK

La Brea Tar Pits &
Page Museum

L.A. County
Museum of Art

Dodger Stadium

Chinatown

El Pueblo de Los Angeles
State Historic Park

MONTEREY
PARK

SANTA
MONICA

Century
City

LOS ANGELES

Music
Center

Little Tokyo
City Hall

Malibu

Wells Fargo
History Museum

Museum of
Contemporary Art

EAST LOS
ANGELES

CULVER
CITY

Exposition Park
(California Museum
of Science & Industry
/Los Angeles County
Natural History
Museum)

Memorial
Coliseum

MONTEBELLO

VENICE

Marina
del
Rey

PLAYA DEL REY

INGLEWOOD

HUNTINGTON
PARK

BELL
GARDENS

PICO
RIVERA

Santa Monica
Bay

Los Angeles
International Airport

SOUTH GATE

DOWNEY

LYNWOOD

NORWALK

HAWTHORNE

WILLOWBROOK

COMPTON

PARAMOUNT

BELLFLOWER

MANHATTAN BEACH

GARDENA

CERRITOS

HERMOSA BEACH

LAKEWOOD

REDONDO BEACH

TORRANCE

CARSON

South Coast
Botanic Garden

Palos Verdes
Peninsula

WILMINGTON

LONG
BEACH

RANCHO
PALOS VERDES

Wayfarers'
Chapel

Marineland

SAN
PEDRO

Hotel
Queen Mary

LOS ANGELES

0   5   10 km

0   5 miles

Santa Monica Mountains

San Diego Freeway

Venduro Mountains

Santa Monica Freeway

Harbor Freeway

San Diego Freeway

Long Beach Freeway

San Gabriel River

Los Angeles River

Coyote Creek

San Pedro
Bay

HUNTINGTON
BEACH

San Gabriel Mountains
Angeles National Forest
San Gabriel Reservoir
Morris Reservoir
MONROVIA
Arboretum
AZUSA
GLENDORA
ARCADIA
TEMPLE CITY
BALDWIN PARK
COVINA
EL MONTE
SAN BERNADINO FREEWAY
WEST COVINA
San Jose Hills
LA PUENTE
POMONA FREEWAY
Hills
WHITTIER
Puente
LA HABRA
LA MIRADA
FULLERTON
Movieland Wax Museum
BUENA PARK
Knott's Berry Farm
CYPRESS
ANAHEIM
Disneyland
Anaheim Stadium
ORANGE
GARDEN GROVE
WESTMINSTER
Bowers Museum
SANTA ANA
FOUNTAIN VALLEY
Movieland of the Air

MALIBU

J Paul Getty Museum

The J Paul Getty Museum has eclipsed the beach and surfers as the reason for visiting Malibu. High on the rocky Malibu coastal mountains, this extravagant replica of the Roman villa owned by Julius Caesar's father houses one of the world's most priceless collections of art. The antiquarian art collection is particularly strong, with a large number of outstanding Greek and Roman sculptures. Overall the collection is quite eclectic, covering several centuries of painting and drawing, as well as illuminated manuscripts, 19th- and 20th-century American and European photography, furniture and porcelain.

Parking at the museum is limited and it is advisable to book in advance if possible. During the height of the season and at weekends it may be necessary to book as far as two weeks in advance and *must* be made at least one week in advance.

Public transport to the museum is limited. There is an infrequent bus from Santa Monica or you can go by taxi from Malibu.

17985 Pacific Coast Highway, Malibu (tel: 213 458 2003). Open: Tuesday to Sunday, 10am–5pm. Admission free

MARINA DEL REY

This pleasant seaside neighbourhood lies conveniently close to both Los Angeles International Airport and downtown Los Angeles.

There is not really any sightseeing here, but overlooking the Marina del Rey harbour is Fisherman's Village. Its colourful Cape Cod-style buildings house speciality shops and restaurants which are open daily all year round.

Beach Life

The most sought-after houses on the southern coast of California face the beach – no matter that the fog rolls in and the ocean is cold.

The beach plays a major part in the lives of Californians. From Malibu down to Laguna, whatever the weather, on any day of the week, people will be using this narrow strip of sand between the land and the sea.

Surfers are always searching for the perfect waves and often find them north of Malibu. Anglers use every structure that juts into the sea to cast their lines. Joggers jog and skateboarders skate.

At Santa Monica and Venice, the weekend brings out a veritable circus of performers. Jugglers, people on roller skates, weight lifters and fast-food vendors are all

Mission Beach
Broadwalk

Venice Beach

out in force competing for the ever-present audience.

Muscle Beach, just to the north of Venice, is a popular place to watch the blond gods of the Pacific coast pumping iron and impressing the girls.

The girls are no less backward at impressing the boys, skating along the boardwalks in the skimpiest of bikinis.

Volleyball is played in earnest wherever there is an open stretch of sand. Hermosa Beach has a televised world volleyball championship every summer.

Not all the beaches are pretty. Huntington Beach has ugly oil derricks along the coast and offshore, and this hunger for offshore oil is a topic of considerable environmental controversy.

In the northern part of the state the beaches are more popular with the rugged outdoor enthusiasts. Here, waves continually crash on to the rocky coastline and cold winds blow in from the Pacific Ocean. It may be the sunny state of California but this northern coast has a true northern climate.

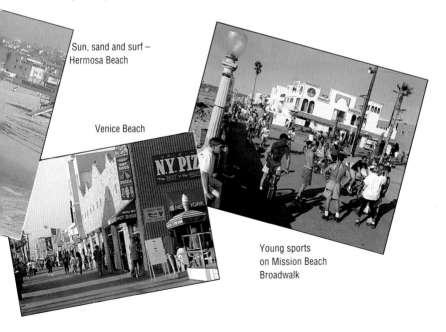

Sun, sand and surf – Hermosa Beach

Venice Beach

Young sports on Mission Beach Broadwalk

NBC Studios at Burbank

MUSEUM OF CONTEMPORARY ART (MOCA)

It may be surprising that what must surely be one of the most trendy cities on earth did not have a museum devoted exclusively to contemporary art until 1986.

It had been hoped to open the new museum in time for the 1984 Olympics but when this was obviously not going to happen, a temporary gallery was opened that proved to be so popular that it is still in use. The Temporary Contemporary, as it is called, is located at 152 North Central Avenue, and a free shuttle service operates between the two facilities.

The museum has a small permanent collection of works from the major modern movements, particularly artists that have worked in California such as Mark Rothko and Clyfford Still. The museum regularly features travelling exhibits.

The museum as a building is worth seeing in itself. The red sandstone and glass building was designed by Japanese architect Arata Isozaki.
250 South Grand Avenue, Los Angeles (tel: 213 626 6222).
Open: Tuesday, Wednesday, Friday and weekends, 11am–6pm; Thursday, 11am–8pm. Admission charge. Free Thursday, 5pm–8pm

MUSIC CENTER

Three performance spaces are combined into this impressive complex: the Dorothy Chandler Pavilion, which is home to the Civic Light Opera and the Los Angleles Philharmonic Orchestra; the Mark Taper Forum, a theatre for contemporary drama; and the Ahmanson Theatre, a 2000-seat auditorium for traditional drama.
135 North Grand Avenue, Los Angeles (tel: 213 972 7211).
Free tours are offered in English, Spanish and French. Call for information.

NBC STUDIOS

Most of the major film and television studios have relocated to Burbank in the San Fernando Valley.

NBC no longer give public tours of the studios, but free TV show tickets are available and must be requested at least two weeks in advance.
3000 West Alameda Avenue, Burbank (tel: 818 840 3537).

OLD TOWN

Close to the heart of modern Los Angeles there still remains a block of buildings dating back to the birth of the city. The Pueblo de Los Angeles State Historic Park preserves this historic area that was first settled in 1781.

The Avila Adobe is the oldest building in Los Angeles and was constructed around 1818. It is open to the public. The other buildings line

either side of Olvera Street, a pedestrianised way that is a permanent Mexican marketplace with craft shops and cafés almost obscuring the historic buildings behind. It gives a strong flavour of early Spanish California.
El Pueblo de Los Angeles Historic Park, 845 North Alemeda Street, Los Angeles (tel: 213 628 1274).
Free walking tours start at 130 Paseo de la Rosa from Tuesday to Saturday on the hour, from 10am to 1pm. Shops open weekdays until 8pm.

PASADENA

Pasadena came to prominence in the late 1900s because of its agreeable climate. Only 20 minutes by freeway from downtown Los Angeles, the town sits at the foot of the San Gabriel Mountains.

Driving around the town will give a good impression of past and present wealth, with many very fine houses on tree-lined avenues.

The historic centre of the town has been restored over the last few years and, in a 10-block area known as 'Old Town', pawn shops and adult book stores are gradually giving way to art galleries and trendy restaurants. Fortunately the original Victorian façades are being preserved.

Huntington Library and Art Gallery

It would be difficult to find a more impressive collection of paintings and manuscripts anywhere.

Of the four million items in the library, several are of unique value. The Ellesmere Manuscript from Chaucer's *Canterbury Tales* dates back to 1410. There is a two-volume Gutenberg Bible printed on parchment in 1455, a Shakespeare Folio edition and Audubon's original edition of *Birds of*

America. The collection of American art is impressive, but you will also find Gainsborough's *Blue Boy* and Thomas Lawrence's *Pinkie* among the paintings.

As if all this is not enough, the grounds of the Huntington match the galleries in interest, with several different gardens, each devoted to a different theme. The Japanese Garden is the most popular, but there is also a herb garden, rose garden, subtropical garden and a Shakespeare garden with only plants that existed in the playwright's time. There are guided tours through the gardens every day at 1pm.

The $3^1/_2$-hour opening time is unrealistic to do justice to this collection and it is worth getting there early. Sundays can be very crowded.
1151 Oxford Road, San Marino (tel: 818 405 2100).
Open: Tuesday to Friday, 1pm–4.30pm; Saturday and Sunday, 10.30am–4.30pm. Admission charge

Norton Simon Museum of Art

This unusual modern group of building houses a collection of art spanning 2,500 years. It is an impressive collection with paintings by Rembrandt, Raphael and Rubens; drawings by Goya; sculpture by Rodin and Henry Moore; and works by Cézanne, Van Gogh and Dégas.

The biggest display is of French art, from Poussin and Wateau through to the Impressionists and on to the Cubists, with important works by most of the major artists of each movement. One whole gallery is devoted to 88 works by Dégas, and the museum has countless models for his bronze figures.
411 West Colorado Boulevard, Pasadena (tel: 818 449 6840).
Open: Thursday to Sunday, noon–6pm. Admission charge

Shades of Santa Monica

SANTA MONICA

Santa Monica is a beach town with one of the best piers in California as its focus.

Here you will find the California of the Beach Boys. Bronzed surfers, body-builders working out, and every kind of performer and musician. On the beach, just by the pier, volleyball courts are in constant use, even late into the night.

The pier itself has a multitude of shops, a couple of restaurants, a turn-of-the-century roundabout with hand-painted horses that were featured in *The Sting*, more modern dodgem cars, shooting galleries, pinball arcades and all manner of Californian characters to complete the scene.

It is worth spending an hour or two strolling around the beach and pier to get the flavour of laid-back southern California.

SOUTHWEST MUSEUM

The native American Indians are the subject of this museum housed in a mission-style building high above downtown Los Angeles.

Good collection of jewellery, basketwork and weaving by the Pueblo Indian tribes form the core of the collection, but the focus is now on all Native Americans, rather than just those from the southwest as the museum's name implies.

234 Museum Drive, Los Angeles (tel: 213 221 2163). Open: Tuesday to Saturday, 11am–5pm; Sunday 1pm–5pm. Admission charge

UNIVERSAL STUDIOS

A tour of Universal Studios should be very high on the list of every first-time visitor to Los Angeles.

This is as close to 'Hollywood' as most people will ever be able to get. It is, however, a Hollywood version of 'Tinsel Town'.

The half-day tour takes you through the backlots covering 420 acres with 36 sound stages and over 10,000 film-makers. Many of the scenes on the tour are instantly recognisable by film buffs: the *Psycho* house, streets of façades used for any number of Westerns, the 1920s street that was the location for *The Sting*, they are all here.

As interesting as this behind-the-scenes experience are the special attractions, which are the most memorable. Where else is it possible to experience the full magnitude of an 8.3 earthquake while on an underground train with water mains bursting all around, and still live to tell the tale?

The effects are quite incredible, and just from the engineering point of view they are well worth the admission fee. Within an hour the visitor will have an encounter with King Kong, an attack by Jaws, and witness a parting of the Red Sea, before being on the verge of getting washed away by a flash flood.

After the tour there is a choice of several different shows, including Star Trek Adventure with audience participation, the Miami Vice Action spectacular, 'Riot Act' stunt show, the Adventures of Conan, or you can wander around The Streets of the World which is like one huge film set.
100 Universal City Plaza, Universal City. Hollywood Freeway exit Linkershim Boulevard (tel: 818 508 9600). Open: Monday to Friday, 9am–5pm in the summer, 10am–3.30pm rest of the year; Saturday and Sunday, 9.30am–3.30pm. Admission charge

VENICE

The best way to describe Venice is funky. Walking along the boardwalk you will be passed by just about every form of pedestrian-powered wheeled transport in existence – roller skates, bicycles, monocycles, skateboards, along with the usual array of joggers and surfers on their way to 'catch the big one'.

In the summer the beach is packed with sun worshippers and the parking problem becomes a nightmare.

At all times of year there is plenty of activity. Up near 18th Avenue is Muscle Beach where aspiring Arnold Schwarzeneggers can be watched pumping iron while at the southern end of town is a 1,100-foot-long pier.

Only three blocks away from all this activity is the small area of tranquil canals that gave Venice its name (see **Walk 1**).

Universal Studios

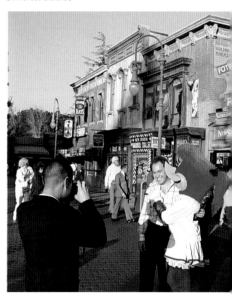

San Diego

San Diego is the ideal vacation destination. The climate is superb with warm, sunny days which the Pacific breezes prevent from getting too hot. It rarely rains (a problem for residents but not for visitors), it never freezes, and the average annual daytime temperature range is between 14°C (58°F) and 21°C (70°F). It has 70 miles of sandy beaches and plenty of attractions, including what is considered to be the world's finest zoo and an enormous natural harbour, and is a cultural centre of some significance.

The waterfront at San Diego

Most of the two and a half million residents of San Diego County live within 30 miles of the ocean and the sea plays a major role in everyday life. This is the headquarters of the 11th Naval District and provides a home for one of the world's largest fleets of fighting ships. It is also home for the America's Cup, the prestigious sailing trophy.

There is history too. This is the birthplace of California. Father Junípero Serra established his first mission here in 1769 but over 200 years before that the Portugese explorer Juan Rodríguez Cabrillo landed in what is now San Diego Bay and claimed it for Spain. The 'Old Town' has been made into a State Historic Park.

Mexico is on the doorstep. Just 20 miles from downtown San Diego and you are in Tijuana across the border – but remember to take your passport, and non-US citizens will need to produce a multiple entry visa.

San Diego is only 120 miles south of Los Angeles and it is an easy 2- to 3-hour drive depending on the traffic. The international airport must be one of the most convenient in the world, being situated only 3 miles from the heart of the city. Downtown hotels can be reached within minutes of leaving the airport.

In spite of being the sixth largest city in the United States and California's second biggest city with a population of over one million, it still has the feel of a much smaller town. Maybe this is because the road system is so good or because the major attractions are relatively close together. Whatever the reason, there never seems to be the pressure of time that occurs in Los Angeles.

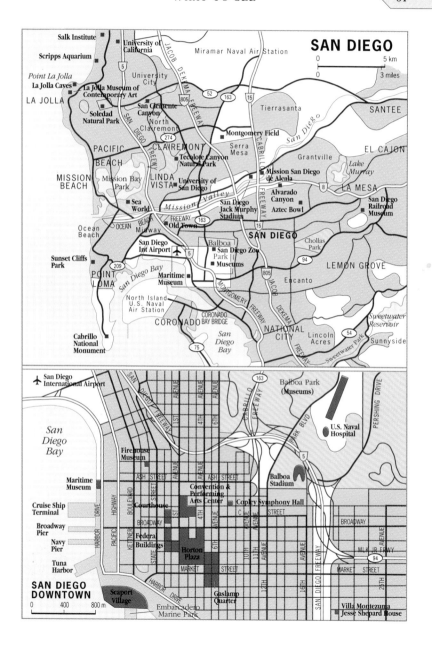

SAN DIEGO

Salk Institute
Scripps Aquarium
University of California
Miramar Naval Air Station
Point La Jolla
La Jolla Caves
La Jolla Museum of Contemporary Art
LA JOLLA
University City
Soledad Natural Park
San Clemente Canyon
North Clairemont
TIERRASANTA
SANTEE
San Diego
PACIFIC BEACH
CLAIREMONT
Serra Mesa
Montgomery Field
Grantville
EL CAJON
MISSION BEACH
Tecolote Canyon Natural Park
LINDA VISTA
University of San Diego
Mission San Diego de Alcala
Lake Murray
LA MESA
Mission Bay Park
Sea World
Alvarado Canyon
San Diego Jack Murphy Stadium
Aztec Bowl
San Diego Railroad Museum
Ocean Beach
OCEAN BEACH
Midway
Old Town
SAN DIEGO
Chollas Park
San Diego Int Airport
Balboa Park
San Diego Zoo
Museums
Sunset Cliffs Park
LEMON GROVE
POINT LOMA
Maritime Museum
San Diego Bay
Encanto
North Island U.S. Naval Air Station
CORONADO BAY BRIDGE
San Diego Bay
CORONADO
NATIONAL CITY
Lincoln Acres
Sweetwater Reservoir
Cabrillo National Monument
Sunnyside

SAN DIEGO DOWNTOWN

San Diego International Airport
San Diego Bay
Firehouse Museum
Balboa Park (Museums)
U.S. Naval Hospital
PERSHING DRIVE
Maritime Museum
ASH STREET
Convention & Performing Arts Center
Balboa Stadium
Copley Symphony Hall
Cruise Ship Terminal
Courthouse
BROADWAY
Broadway Pier
Federal Buildings
Horton Plaza
MARKET STREET
Navy Pier
Tuna Harbor
Scaport Village
Gaslamp Quarter
Villa Montezuma
Jesse Shepard House
Embarcadero Marine Park
0   400   800 m

BALBOA PARK
(see also **Walk 2**)

Botanical Building
Right in the centre of the park, behind the lily pond, is a building that looks like a huge overturned basket. In fact, the steel framework was made for a station belonging to the Santa Fe Railroad, but was purchased for the 1915 Exposition.

It now houses a large collection of ferns and other tropical and subtropical plants.
Tel: 619 236 5717.
Open: daily, except Fridays, 10am–4pm.

California Tower
This 200-foot-high landmark structure was the centrepiece for the 1915 Panama–California Exposition. Its Spanish Renaissance architecture still dominates the main thoroughfare of Balboa Park. Immediately below it is the Museum of Man.

The tower houses a 100-bell carillon that chimes every quarter-hour.

Museum of Photographic Arts
The museum is one of the few in North America devoted exclusively to photography. A small gallery has regular exhibitions of prints by major photographers, and an excellent shop has a wide range of publications on photography.
Tel: 619 239 5262. Open: daily,
10am–5pm; Thursdays, until 9pm.
Admission charge

Old Globe Theater
The San Diego Repertory Company makes its home in this re-creation of Shakespeare's original Globe Theatre in London.

It was originally built for the 1935 California–Pacific International Exhibition, burned down in 1978, and was reconstructed, winning a coveted Tony Award for its stage.

Adjoining the Globe are the **Lowell Davies Festival Theater** and the **Simon Edison Center for the Performing Arts** (tel: 619 239 2255).

Reuben H Fleet Space Theater and Science Center
The Space Theater is California's only Omnimax theatre presenting spectacular films on a hemispherical screen that envelopes the audience, making them feel part of the action. State-of-the-art sound is delivered by 152 separate speakers. It also features one of the largest planetariums in the country.

The Science Center is a hands-on exhibit, essentially for children, covering the laws of science.
Tel: 619 238 1168.
Open: daily, 9.30am–9.30pm.
Admission charge

San Diego Aerospace Museum
The whole history of aviation is covered in this circular building. From a replica of the 'Spirit of St Louis' to the latest spacecraft and everything in between, including modern fighter aircraft in the centre courtyard of the museum.

There are over 70 aircraft, spacecraft and associated artefacts in the collection. The exhibits unfold in a chronological fashion starting with the Montgolfier brothers' hot-air balloon and ending with America's current Space Shuttle programme. Every aspect of aviation is covered including an extensive exhibit on the role of women in aviation.

Alongside the main exhibits is the **International Aerospace Hall of Fame**. The Hall of Fame concept is

popular throughout the US, and in this museum it is nothing more than a collection of annotated photographs of the great men and women in the history of aerospace.
Tel: 619 234 8291. Open: daily, 10am–4.30pm. Admission charge

San Diego Automotive Museum
Situated next door to the Aerospace Museum, this museum has a display of over 80 vehicles including horseless carriages, brass cars, performance and exotic cars, and future prototypes.
Tel: 619 231 2544. Open: daily. Admission charge

San Diego Model Railroad Museum
In the basement of the same building as the Museum of Photographic Arts you can discover the world's largest collection of mini-gauge trains.

Scenes of San Diego and southern California have been reduced to scale to provide a landscape for the trains to journey through.
Tel: 619 696 0199. Open: Wednesday to Friday, 11am–4pm; Saturday and Sunday, 11am–5pm. Admission charge

San Diego Museum of Art
Although this is not one of the great art museums of the world there is a good collection that is particularly strong on Flemish and pre-Renaissance painting.

Adjoining the museum is a sculpture garden with a small but excellent collection by artists such as Calder, Miró, Hepworth and Moore.

As with many of the buildings in Balboa Park, the architecture is as interesting as the exhibits. The façade of the Museum of Art is a copy of the 17th-century University of Salamanca in Spain.

San Diego Aerospace Museum

Tel: 619 232 7931. Open: Tuesday to Sunday, 10am–4.30pm. Admission charge

San Diego Museum of Man
At the core of the collection are artefacts collected from the Pueblo Indians of the southwest and the Aztec and Mayan settlements of Latin America by the Smithsonian Institution in Washington.

There is now a broader anthropological base to the museum, highlighting man's physical and cultural development. In addition, there are frequent special exhibits from Pacific Rim cultures.
Tel: 619 239 2001. Open: daily 10am–4.30pm. Admission charge

San Diego Natural History Museum
The environment of southern California is the main emphasis of this 100-year-old institution. There are the usual dioramas of the Californian coast and a topical exhibit called 'On the Edge', which focuses on rare and endangered plants and animals.

As with many of the museums in Balboa Park, the building is almost more impressive than its contents.
Tel: 619 232 3821. Open: daily, 10am–4.30pm. Admission charge

San Diego Zoo

This is often considered to be the world's greatest zoo, and for very good reasons.

In a time when zoos are falling both out of favour and out of business, San Diego Zoo is a remarkable success.

For one thing it is big and covers 128 acres. There is a lot of space for the animals, and there are a lot of animals – 3,900 from 800 species. An effort has been made to concentrate on endangered species and to develop breeding programmes for these animals.

The site of the zoo extends across a steep canyon and to tour the zoo on foot involves some serious walking. This is certainly the best way to make the most of the exhibits, but for those unable to cope with the steep gradients there is a 3-mile double-decker-bus tour through the zoo which also provides an informative commentary.

Yet another aspect of the zoo can be found by taking a trip in the **Skyfari** aerial tram for a bird's-eye view above the treetops.

Some of the world's rarest and most interesting primates are on display here, and a recently opened gorilla exhibit – the **Gorilla Tropics** – re-creates over 2.5 acres of the habitat that is the home for six lowland gorillas.

Also of interest is a rainforest complete with artifical mist, a large collection of koala bears from Australia and tiny pygmy chimpanzees from central Africa.
Tel: 619 234 3153. Open: daily 9am–5pm. Admission charge

Spreckels Organ

Every Sunday at 2pm a recital is given on this giant among organs. It was given to the city in 1915 by the sons of millionaire Adolf Spreckels and remains the biggest open-air organ in the world. The longest pipes are almost 33 feet in length.

Spanish Village Arts and Crafts Center

Leaving the zoo and entering the Prado area of Balboa Park you will pass a group of low, Spanish-style buildings where craftsmen and artists are busy at work turning out a variety of souvenirs for visitors.

This is very much a commercial venture but occasionally interesting work can be found here.
Tel: 619 234 4111.
Open: daily, 11am–4pm.

CORONADO

The exclusive community of Coronado is almost an island. A long, narrow sand bar known as the Silver Strand connects it to the mainland. Until 1969 the only access was by ferry or a very long drive but then the San Diego–Coronado Bay Bridge was built, and now it only takes a few minutes to drive there from downtown San Diego.

Coronado has the ambience of a different era. Although it is now only minutes from the busy centre of San Diego it is like being in a quaint village. The affluence of the community is reflected in the immaculate tree-lined avenues and expensive houses but, pleasant as it must be to live there, there is not a lot for the visitor to do.

The main attraction is the **Hotel del Coronado**. This is one of the great hotels of the world, built of wood in 1888 and still in use as a luxury hotel. Thomas Edison personally supervised the installation of electricty in the hotel, which at the time was the only building

SAN DIEGO SAFARI
The San Diego Zoo's
Wild Animal Park re-
creates both Asian
and African habitats
on its 1,800-acre site.
Over 2,500 animals
roam free as they are
viewed from elevated
walkways or on a 50-
minute tour on the
Wgasa Bush Line
monorail.

*The park lies 35 miles
to the north of San
Diego off I-15.
15500 San Pasqual
Valley Road,
Escondido (tel: 619
234 6541).
Open: daily.
Admission charge*

Water beating at San Diego Zoo

outside New York to be fully served with electricity.

Twelve American presidents have stayed there and it has been made a National Historic Landmark. It was featured in the film *Some Like It Hot* and the management make great play of this, but even without the Hollywood connection the hotel is worth a visit.

Wander around the beautifully kept grounds and down to the beach.

Unfortunately most of the beach area along the Silver Strand has been used for military manoeuvres, and warning notices make it quite clear that the area is out of bounds.

GASLAMP QUARTER

In the 1800s this was San Diego's main street area. At the turn of the century it became a flourishing red-light district. It is in the heart of modern San Diego and, like many inner-city areas, it suffered a long period of neglect.

San Diego's Gaslamp Quarter

A concerted effort has been made to restore the district to its original glory and it has been designated a National Historic District. Many of the buildings have now been renovated. The area still has not been able to shake off its somewhat seedy image but now the pawnshops rub shoulders with trendy new restaurants and antique shops.

There are several very fine examples of Victorian architecture and the Gaslamp Quarter Foundation at 410 Island Avenue can provide a free, detailed map of the district with histories of the individual buildings. They also offer tours on Saturdays at 11am. A small donation to the foundation is expected.
Broadway to Harbor Drive between
4th and 6th avenues (tel: 619 233 5227).

HORTON PLAZA

This colourful, modern shopping plaza that opened in 1985 is the centre-piece for the new downtown area of San Diego. It is a textbook example of good design. The human scale and visually stimulating architecture combine with first-rate shops to make shopping here a totally satisfying experience. Even if you hate shopping it is still worth walking through the plaza just for the pleasure of the building. How many shopping malls can you say that about?

On the upper level of the plaza are a wide range of restaurants and cafés serving food from all over the world and in every price range. You will also find here a seven-screen cinema and two performing arts theatres.
Broadway and G Street.

LA JOLLA

Residents of this ritzy community of San Diego like to think of their neighbourhood as a separate entity and refer to it as 'The Village'. Even the post office stamps mail La Jolla although it is part of the city of San Diego.

La Jolla (pronounced 'La Hoya') is not unlike an exclusive Mediterranean resort with the same mix of expensive houses, exquisite boutiques, gourmet restaurants and grand hotels. The cliff-

Futuristic Horton Shopping Plaza

A friendly Pacific Octopus at the Scripps
Institution Aquarium, La Jolla

lined coast adds to this impression.

It is the perfect place to walk. The
scale is intimate which makes driving
around difficult at best. The landmark
building in town is the pink **La Valencia
Hotel** which has long been a popular
retreat for the Hollywood set.

The Salk Institute
Spectacularly located high on the edge of
a canyon overlooking the Pacific, the
Salk Institute was established by polio
vaccine discoverer Jonas Salk as an
environment that would stimulate
original thinking. The surreal concrete
building that houses the Institute was
designed by Louis Kahn in 1960.
*Tours of the Instutute can be arranged in
advance by calling 619 453 4100, extension
200. 10010 North Torre Pines Road,
San Diego.*

Scripps Aquarium
The best beaches in town stretch north
of La Jolla up to the Scripps Institution
of Oceanography, which is part of the
University of California.

The aquarium here displays the
marine life of the Pacific, both in tanks
and in an on-shore tidepool, together
with displays of the latest advances in
oceanography.
*8602 La Jolla Shores Drive, San Diego
(tel: 619 534 6933).*

University of California, San Diego
The beautiful UCSD campus just to
the north of the Scripps Aquarium
has an internationally acclaimed
collection of commissioned site-specific
sculpture.

Walking tours are given and
brochures are available at the UCSD
information kiosks at the Gilman Drive
and North Torre Pines Road entrances
(tel: 619 534 3120).

MARITIME MUSEUM OF SAN DIEGO

This rather grandiose name is given to three ships moored on the Embarcadero.

The *Star of India* built in 1863 is the oldest iron-hulled ship in America that is still afloat. Also here is the San Francisco Bay ferry-boat, *Berkeley,* which played a major role in evacuating victims of the 1906 earthquake, and a 1904 steam yacht, the *Medea,* which still makes occasional trips around San Diego Bay.

1306 North Harbor Drive, San Diego (tel: 619 234 9153). Open: daily, 9am–8pm. Admission charge

MISSION BAY PARK

If it can be done on water, it can be done on San Diego's Mission Bay. This city-owned aquatic park is the biggest of its kind in the world.

Each watersport has its own designated area. There are six public swimming areas, which are off limits to boats. Water-skiers have their own 1.5 mile straight course and jet-skiers also have their own special area free from boat traffic.

At most of the bay's marinas you can buy, rent or charter almost anything that floats, from a kayak to a skiing speedboat. Sailing and windsurfing lessons are also available at reasonable rates.

Landlubbers can rent bicycles for leisurely rides along the many bike trails over the 4,600 acres and there are over 20 miles of running paths for joggers and walkers.

For the less active there are plenty of fish to be caught, and tackle can be rented by the day.

For the non-active there is not too much sightseeing. The landscape is flat and is not significantly different from watersports areas in other places. There is, however, one attraction that never fails to impress visitors of any age.

Sea World

This is the marine equivalent of Disneyland, a fantasy land inhabited by all forms of marine life. This 135-acre park features six major shows that are alternately staged throughout the day at stadiums and indoor auditoriums. Between shows, one can touch or view live animals at 20 educational exhibits

---

MARITIME MATTERS

San Diego has always had close ties with the sea. During World War II, the Korean War and the Vietnam War the city was home to the Pacific Fleet. It is very much a 'navy town' and by 1986 it had the largest concentration of naval power in the western world. There were 110,000 uniformed personnel stationed there, about 20 per cent of the entire US Navy.

The 'Top Gun' attack fighter school is here too, at NAS Miramar.

Every weekend, as a reminder of its presence in San Diego, the Navy docks a vessel at the Broadway Pier for the public to visit.

In recent years, San Diego has been associated with the America's Cup, the oldest trophy in international sport. In 1987, the San Diego based *Stars and Stripes* won the cup back from Australia. The America's Cup Museum at B Street Pier, Cruise Ship Terminal (tel: 619 685 1412), is open daily, 10am–6pm.

and four aquariums.

Sea World really deserves a whole day to do it justice but if time is limited there are two shows that must not be missed.

The number one attraction is without doubt Baby Shamu, a young killer whale born in the park. The **Shamu Show** in the Shamu Stadium is a must. The other not-to-be-missed production is **Pirates of Pinniped** starring a talented troupe of sea lions, otters and a spitting walrus.

Of the exhibits, the **Dolphin Pool** is always very popular and a true encounter experience. The dolphins love to be petted by the visitors. Similarly the **Penguin Encounter**, where you can watch the largest penguin colony north of the Antarctic, never fails to please.

For a different perspective of the park take either the Southwest Skytower or the Skyride to give you a bird's-eye view of both Sea World and the whole of Mission Bay.

1720 South Shores Road, San Diego (tel: 619 226 3901). Admission charge

The Dolphin Pool at Sea World, a perennial favourite with young and old alike. Sea World, like Disneyland, has created a clone in Orlando, Florida

The Mission at San Diego

MISSION VALLEY

Considering the historic importance of Father Junípero Serra's first mission in California, **Mission San Diego de Alcala** is in a curiously suburban setting. The mission is really the only site of interest in the valley and is refreshingly uncommercial.

The original mission was built in 1769 but was moved a few years later because of disputes between the Spanish and the Indians. The second mission was burned down by the Indians in 1775 and the present mission was constructed in 1777. Destroyed by an earthquake in 1803, all that remains now is a church with a bell tower and a small museum

set in beautiful gardens.
10818 San Diego Mission Road, San Diego (tel: 619 281 8449). Open: daily, 9am–5pm. Admission charge

OLD TOWN

Old Town is where San Diego began; it was the first European settlement in California.

The State of California bought six blocks of historic buildings in the 1960s and established the Old Town State Historic Park in 1967. The core of the park is a traditional Mexican plaza around which many of the old buildings are located. Altogether there are 16 historic structures of which 10 house museums – there are also 33 craft and specialty shops and seven restaurants!

This commercial element tends to be concentrated on the **Bazaar del Mundo**, a loud and garish shopping and restaurant complex immediately off the main plaza. Fortunately most of the visitors tend to congregate here, leaving the rest of the park relatively quiet, and thus preserving the historic atmosphere of the area.

A self-guided walking tour brochure is available free of charge at the Visitor Center in the **Robinson Rose House**, or free guided tours are available every day at 2pm outside the Visitor Center.
Old Town San Diego State Historic Park, 4002 Wallace Street, San Diego (tel: 619 237 6770). Museums open weekends, 10am–5pm.

POINT LOMA

A drive out to the **Cabrillo National Monument** at Point Loma is worth it if only for the view. On a clear day there is a sweeping view from La Jolla all the way to Mexico.

During the winter this is the ideal

place to watch hundreds of California grey whales on their annual migration from Alaska to their breeding grounds off the coast of Baja California in Mexico.

The museum here is only of passing interest and in itself would barely justify the 10-mile drive out from San Diego. The nearby statue of Cabrillo is equally unimpressive.

The restored **Old Point Loma Lighthouse** is a short walk away and open for visits. For hikers, there are plenty of trails down to the shore of the peninsula.

To reach Point Loma from San Diego take Rosencrans Street to Catalina Boulevard and then follow Cabrillo Memorial Drive until you

arrive at the monument.

SEAPORT VILLAGE

This modern shopping and dining complex, only a few minutes walk from the very heart of downtown San Diego, is intended to depict the harbourside as it was a century ago. It is difficult to believe that it could have been so well manicured back then, but it does provide a very agreeable environment for shopping with pleasant landscaped walks overlooking the harbour.

Some 14 acres have been developed with over 60 shops and 17 restaurants, and there are ambitious extension works planned.

San Diego Old Town

Desert Life

Mention 'the desert' to anyone in Los Angeles and they will immediately conjure up images of rolling green golf courses.

The fact that most of the southern half of California is desert is not enough to overshadow the importance of Palm Springs. This incongruous oasis of hedonism certainly has a major economic significance; it is certainly not 'the desert'.

Inevitably it was gold that was the lure into this inhospitable environment, but paradoxically it was not gold but borax that made the desert millionaires. Today the biggest borax mine in the world is at Boron near Mojave where 10,000 tons of borax are mined every day.

The desert settlements tend to be small, messy little towns with very little aesthetic appeal. Most of them have developed alongside local industries.

At Daggett, close to Barstow, is Solar One, the world's biggest solar energy plant. Hundreds of mirrors set out in concentric circles on the desert floor track the sun and direct the heat on to a central receptor which in turn generates steam to drive turbines.

Mojave has long been associated with the US Air Force and NASA programmes and nearby Edwards Air Force Base is the preferred landing strip for the Challenger space shuttle.

The real interest in the desert, however, is in the dramatic landscapes, unique vegetation and wildlife.

Plant life abounds and although much of it is dormant for most of the year, for a few weeks in the

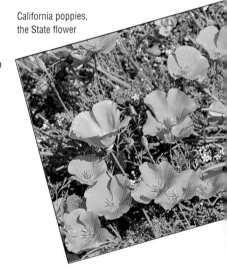

California poppies, the State flower

spring the desert becomes a blaze of colour. The Mojave Desert begins in Antelope Valley and here the California poppy provides a spectacular display from March until May. During the blooming season there is a special wildflower hotline (tel: 805 724 1180) which gives daily updates.

The desert vegetation ranges from tiny cacti to huge Joshua trees, which are surprisingly members of the lily family. Many of the plants are the habitat of equally abundant wildlife.

During the summer the average daytime temperature in Death Valley is 116°F. Because of these extreme temperatures many of the animals are nocturnal, and you can often catch a fleeting glimpse of a kangaroo rat in car headlights.

During the day you may spot a bighorn sheep or pronghorn antelope or, more easily, a coyote as the sun begins to fade.

Just north of Mojave at California City there is a Desert Tortoise Reserve, the best time to observe them being in the spring when the flowers are blooming. Throughout the desert country keep an eye open for rattlesnakes, particularly in the early morning when they are sluggish and easily stepped on.

It's all done with mirrors at Doggett

Solar One at Doggett

The Deserts

No visitor to California should leave without experiencing at least one visit to the desert.

In the southern part of the state the desert is all around you and within a couple of hours' drive from almost anywhere you can be in the middle of an arid wilderness.

Much of the desert is a flat, barren, dusty landscape with little to commend it to the visitor. However, there are large areas of great beauty and interest that have been designated as national or state parks. The best time to visit the deserts is between late autumn and mid-May when temperatures are at their most comfortable level. Summer can be sizzling but because the air is so dry it is rarely totally unbearable and the evenings are always cool and sometimes cold.

Even when driving on main roads it is always a good idea to take water with you in case of a breakdown. You may well need it in the heat, as in many places traffic is infrequent at best.

ANZA-BORREGO

This is one of the largest state parks in the continental US. Over 1,000 square miles of badlands and mountains extend from the Colorado Desert to the great Sonoran Desert across the border in Mexico.

The desert was first crossed by Spanish explorer Juan Bautista de Anza in 1774 and he was commemorated by having his name added to Borrego, Spanish for the bighorn sheep now only found in the more remote corners of the park.

This is not a place for fast sightseeing. There are over 600 miles of roads, mostly unmetalled, and as many footpaths. The best way to experience Anza-Borrego is to explore on foot. Nature walks are led by rangers from the visitor centre during weekends and holidays in season.

Anza-Borrego – beauty and the beast

The variety of desert plants is the highlight of the park and there are several walks that show a good cross-section in a short distance. Particularly notable are the California fan palms, ocotillos, smoke trees and the elephant tree which is unique to Anza-Borrego in North America.

If you have the energy to climb some of the steeper trails, you will be rewarded with magnificent diplays of several varieties of cactus.

Plant life at Anza-Borrego

DESERT WILDLIFE
To the casual visitor the desert regions may appear barren and empty but the California deserts are far from deserted.

Seventy-five species of mammal make their home here and of these, two-thirds are rodents which have most successfully adapted to the desert habitat. Larger mammals include the kit fox, the coyote and bighorn sheep.

The extreme temperatures experienced in the desert regions have forced most mammals to become nocturnal and the best chance of sighting an animal is at dawn or dusk or in the light of car headlamps.

Reptiles are more commonly seen. Several kinds of lizard are found throughout the region, along with five kinds of rattlesnake and the sidewinder (although snakes are by no means a commom sight).

In spring the deserts are alive with birds, and the cheeky roadrunner, of all desert wildlife, symbolises nature's ability to conquer hostile environments.

For a good view of the badlands drive up to Font's Point north of Borrego Palm Canyon.

By car, Anza-Borrego is 1.5 hours south of Palm Springs and 2 hours east of San Diego.

Anza-Borrego Visitor Center
Three miles west of Borrego Springs, at Borrego Palm Canyon, the visitor centre and museum sit buried in the desert. The building is partially underground, covered with cement and 6 feet of sand.

Outside the museum is a comprehensive cactus garden.
Anza-Borrego State Park, PO Box 299, Borrego Springs, California 92004 (tel: 619 767 4205).

Death Valley

In spite of its forbidding name, very few people have actually died here.

It was Christmas Day 1849 when the first white man gazed down at Death Valley.

What has become known as the Death Valley Party consisted of four families and a group of young men. They were on their way from Salt Lake City looking for an easy way across the Sierra Nevada to the newly discovered gold fields in the San Joaquin Valley.

Twenty-six wagons went into Death Valley but only one made it out. One person died and it is said that the valley was given its name when one of the party looked back as they were leaving and said, 'Goodbye, death valley'.

Today Death Valley has over 500 miles of well-maintained roads and nearly all the attractions are only a short walk away.

Death Valley is unique among desert valleys, not only because of its size and variety of scenery, but also because of its extremes.

It has the lowest point in the western hemisphere at 282 feet below sea-level but Telescope Peak rises to over 11,000 feet only a few miles away. Only 60 miles to the west is Mount Whitney, at 14,495 feet, the highest peak in the continental US outside Alaska.

In 1913 a record high air temperature of 134°F was recorded and summer temperatures regularly exceed 120°F, making it one of the hottest places on earth.

Artist's Palette

Just south of Furnace Creek on Highway 178 a dirt road branches off into the Black Mountains. Artist's Drive, as it is called, makes a 9-mile loop through some of the most barren but colourful landscape in the world. Minerals have leached out of the ground and created a breathtaking display of colour splashed across the mountainsides.

Although Artist's Drive is not paved it is well maintained and accessible to two-wheel-drive vehicles.

Badwater

The lowest point in the western hemisphere is only a short walk down from Highway 178. A pond of saline water permanently occupies this depression even in the hottest months, and in the early morning you can see the reflection of Telescope Peak to the west.

There are extensive salt flats just beyond Badwater. Walking out on to them is like entering a crystalline world of dazzling white stretching for as far as the eye can see.

Borax Museum

In Furnace Creek there is an outdoor museum dedicated to the mineral that made fortunes in Death Valley. There is a collection of old stagecoaches, wagons and mining equipment. The oldest house in Death Valley is here, built in 1883.

Two miles north is the Harmony Borax Works, the ruins of the valley's first borax plant. An original 20-mule-team rig, looking as sturdy as it must have done in 1907, stands in front of the ruin.

Dantes View

Twenty-seven miles from Furnace Creek and 5,478 feet high, Dante's View gives a 360° bird's-eye panorama of Death Valley National Monument. Badwater lies one vertical mile below as you gaze out across the desolate landscape.

If you are up here in the early morning or late evening, take along a sweater. The temperature can be 20°F cooler than the valley. Also, look out for tarantulas. In the autumn these big, hairy but generally harmless spiders are out in their hundreds looking for mates, and you can usually see them crossing the road up to Dante's View.

Devil's Golf Course

A dirt road off Highway 190 between Stovepipe Wells and Furnace Creek takes you to strange salt towers and brine pools. The salt here is up to 5 feet thick and almost as pure as table salt.

Dantes View, Death Valley. With less than 2 inches of rain a year, a ground temperature of 165°F has been recorded

Furnace Creek

Nearby springs have enabled Furnace Creek to become not only the geographical but also the commercial centre of Death Valley. Not that there is much here. Two hotels, two campsites, a couple of restaurants and shops and a very large caravan site which in the winter is full of retired people escaping to the sun.

There is also the Death Valley National Monument Visitor Center which has a small museum and information centre. During the summer this air-conditioned retreat can be a very welcome relief.
Tel: 619 786 2331. Open: daily, 8am–5pm throughout the year and until 9pm from November to April.

Scotty's Castle

By far the single biggest visitor attraction in Death Valley is both man-made and totally incongruous.

At the far northern end of the valley, just off Highway 267 close to Ubehebe Crater, a flamboyant rogue and sometime prospector, nicknamed Death Valley Scotty, persuaded Chicago millionaire Albert Johnson to build an extravagant Spanish-style mansion in the desert. Scotty had originally lured Johnson out here with bogus tales of a gold mine. Johnson, however, found that the climate suited his fragile health, forgave Scotty and the two became lifelong friends.

The 25-room house has a 50-foot-high living room, a music room with a 1,600-pipe organ, and even indoor waterfalls that acted as air-conditioners in the summer.

The house is now administered by the National Park Service who give daily tours.

Death Valley National Monument, California 92328 (tel: 619 786 2392). Admission charge

Stovepipe Wells

Although this is the valley's only other town after Furnace Creek it consists of nothing more than a store, motel, restaurant and filling station.

However, 6 miles down the road is a remarkable area of sand dunes. Dawn is the best time to walk into them when the footprints of the previous day's visitors have been blown away and the low dawn light casts long shadows over the sand.

Ubehebe Crater

At the northern end of the park a

Scotty's Castle – baronial splendour some 3,000 feet above the valley floor

volcanic explosion created this huge crater 0.6 miles across and 400 feet deep. A short walk from the car park takes you to the high point on the crater rim with dramatic views of Death Valley against the Black Mountains.

Zabriskie Point
Take Highway 190 for 4 miles east of Furnace Creek and turn off to the Zabriskie Point lookout for one of the best panoramic views of the southern half of Death Valley.

Early morning and late afternoon light is particularly beautiful, and if you have time the best walk in the valley goes from Zabriskie Point down through the badlands, across the foot of Manly Beacon and on through Golden Canyon. The 2.5-mile trail walk takes under 2 hours but you need to arrange for a lift back up to the lookout car park.

JOSHUA TREE NATIONAL MONUMENT
The high Mojave Desert meets the low Colorado Desert here at Joshua Tree.

The park was named for the thousands of spikey, tree-like plants that are actually giant members of the lily family. These 'trees' grow only between the 3,000 to 5,000 foot altitudes and can reach heights of 40 feet.

The most impressive groups of plants are in the high western part of the park. The road passes by enormous, rounded granite boulders that are scattered through the landscape. These provide a platform for gymnastic displays by rock climbers.

There are three entrances to the park, from Highway 62 at Joshua Tree or Twentynine Palms, and in the south, via Cottonwood Springs Road off I-10.

Oasis Visitor Center
The best way to enter the park is from the town of Twentynine Palms. The Visitor Center will supply maps and trail guides as well as brochures and general information. There is also a shop and small museum at this entrance.

Cholla Cactus Garden
Winding down from the Mojave into the Colorado Desert the landscape changes from rugged rocks and mountains into a more barren, flat expanse of parched earth.

The Cholla Cactus Garden is a forest of Opuntia cacti that manages to survive in this harsh environment. One of the prettiest walks in the park passes through here, but be warned. The other name for

Jumping cactuses at the Cholla Garden

the cholla is 'jumping cactus' and with good reason. Although they do not actually jump the plants have an annoying tendency to attach themselves to you with even the slightest touch. They rarely grow higher than 3 feet but the length of their spines makes up for their lack of height! Also keep an eye open for the five types of rattlesnake that live here.

Joshua Tree National Monument, 74485 National Monument Drive, Twentynine Palms, CA 92277 (tel: 619 367 7511). Visitor centres open daily, 8am–4.30pm. Admission charge

PALM SPRINGS

To anyone in southern California 'the desert' means Palm Springs and its equally affluent neighbours, Rancho Mirage and Palm Desert.

Before the 1920s this was a sleepy little health spa where people came for the hot springs and dry air. Then it was discovered by Hollywood.

Palm Springs rapidly grew to become one of the world's major winter resorts. The skies are always blue, the air always clear, and the golf courses, all 84 of them, always green.

There is even cross-country skiing up on Mount San Jacinto, towering 8,600 feet above Palm Springs.

'The Season' for 'the desert' starts in January and continues through to the end of April. To be seen here before Christmas or after Easter is just not done, unless, of course, you want the best rates at hotels and some great travel bargains. The summer can be very hot but the discounts available can almost make the temperatures bearable. However, many attractions close or have limited hours during the summer. Always telephone in advance.

Moorten's Botanical Garden

This 4-acre garden displays over 3,000 different varieties of cactus and other desert plants. You will also see plenty of lizards, birds and dinosaur fossils throughout the garden.
1701 S Palm Canyon Drive, Palm Springs (tel: 619 327 6555). Open: daily, 9am–5pm. Admission charge

Palm Springs Aerial Tramway

A cable car ride to the summit of Mount San Jacinto is one of Palm Springs' most popular attractions. This mile-high ride provides views from Joshua Tree across

to the Salton Sea with the whole of the Palm Springs valley in the foreground.

At the top of the mountain, apart from the usual restaurant, bar and souvenir shops, there is a 0.75 mile nature trail, and mules are available for 20-minute rides around the slopes.

Depending upon snow conditions, usually from late November to mid-April, the Nordic Ski Center is open for cross-country ski excursions.
Aerial Tramway (tel: 619 325 1391). Open: Monday to Friday, 10am–8pm; weekends and holidays, 8am–8pm. Admission charge
San Jacinto Ranger Station (tel: 619 327 0222).
Nordic Ski Center (tel: 619 325 3490).

Palm Springs Desert Museum

This museum has an eclectic assortment of exhibits from western American art to desert natural history to Indian basketry. It is a collection of considerable regional importance and worth a visit if only for the delightfully landscaped sculpture garden.
101 Museum Drive, Palm Springs (tel: 619 325 7186). Open: September to early June, Tuesday to Friday, 10am–4pm; weekends, 10am–5pm. Admission charge

Village Green Heritage Center

In the middle of the exclusive shops and restaurants of **Palm Canyon Drive,** three old buildings from Palm Springs' past look almost too perfect to be genuine.

The **McCallum Adobe** was built in 1884 and is the town's oldest building. Next door is Cornelia White's 1893 home made from railroad ties, and then there is **Ruddy's General Store.**

The store is a re-creation of a typical 1930s general store complete with

shelves stocked with over 6,000 genuine items from the period. It is one of the most complete displays of unused general store merchandise in the country.
221 South Palm Canyon Drive, Palm Springs (tel: 619 323 8297). Open: October to June, Thursday to Sunday, 10am–4pm; July to September, weekends only, 10am–4pm. Admission charge

PALM DESERT
This rival of Palm Springs is rapidly becoming one of the desert's major resort towns. The quality of shops along **El Paseo** is exceptional, equal to that of Rodeo Drive in Los Angeles. The town obviously caters to visitors who do not have to worry too much about money.

Apart from shopping, **The Living Desert** is the other attraction that should not be missed in Palm Desert. This 1,200-acre garden and wild animal park re-creates eight different desert habitats. There is even a display of nocturnal animals in a special enclosure.
47900 South Portola Avenue, Palm Desert (tel: 619 346 5694). Open: daily, 9am–5pm from September to mid-June. Admission charge

RANCHO MIRAGE
The only reason to visit Rancho Mirage is to see how the other half live. This extremely wealthy bedroom community between Palm Springs and Palm Desert is home to Bob Hope and Frank Sinatra – both have streets named after them.

There is little of interest for the visitor – unless Frank invites you over for tea.

SALTON SEA
This vast body of water was formed in 1905 when the Colorado River poured billions of gallons of flood water into this desert area that lies below sea level.

There are no natural outlets and over the years evaporation has concentrated the salinity of the water.

It is a major link in the Pacific Flyway, and thousands of birds use the sea either as a stopover or to spend the winter. One-third of all North America's white pelican population winter here.

Nearby Coachella Valley is the centre of the California date growers, and the roads are lined with alternating date-palm groves and shops selling gift-wrapped dates.

Not Switzerland, but Palm Springs

Highway One
(The Coastal Route)

*F*rom Santa Monica to San Francisco, California Highway 1 hugs the coast all the way and en route passes through some of the finest scenery and interesting towns in the state.

This is certainly the very best way to travel from Los Angeles to San Francisco, and it ranks as one of the finest drives in the nation, sandwiched as it is between mountains and sea.

Los Angeles is the best place to start. The drive gets increasingly interesting and spectacular as you drive north. At least two days should be allocated for this trip, which will allow you time for some brief sightseeing stops. The entries from page 82 to 87 are arranged in the order in which you would meet them on the road.

SANTA BARBARA
Santa Barbara is one of the most beautiful towns in the country. It sits on a curving, sandy bay with the Santa Ynez Mountains as a backdrop. Add to this a near perfect climate and you have

On the lookout for lunch – Stearns Wharf

the closest an American town gets to paradise.

The Spanish named it appropriately *la tierra adorada* – the beloved land. A massive earthquake destroyed the town in 1925 and left the way clear to plan a whole new town based on its Spanish roots. Present-day Santa Barbara is mainly Spanish and mission-style architecture with red tile roofs and a strong Mediterranean flavour. Whitewashed walls and elegant palm trees complete the effect.

It seems, however, that there is always trouble in paradise. In 1989 a devastating fire swept through the hills of Santa Barbara, and there is a continuing water shortage of mammoth proportions.

Nethertheless, none of this has prevented an increasing number of Hollywood stars from settling there.

The first stop in Santa Barbara should be the Visitor Information Center at 1 Santa Barbara Street (tel: 805 965 3021).

Ask for maps of the 'Red Tile Tour' for walkers and the 'Scenic Drive'. The street layout can be confusing and a detailed map of the town is invaluable.

County Courthouse

This Spanish–Moorish castle was built in 1929 and remains the grandest building in town. A visit to the top of the bell tower gives an unparalleled view of Santa Barbara and the bay.
1100 Anacapa Street (tel: 805 962 6464). Open: daily, 9am–5pm. Admission free

El Presidio de Santa Barbara State Historic Park

The site is still being excavated and restored and there are two buildings, El Cuartel and La Cañedo Adobe, that were part of the original Spanish fort

blessed by Father Junípero Serra in 1782. A reconstructed chapel and padre's quarters complete the site.
129 East Cañon Perdido Street (tel: 805 966 9719). Open: Monday to Friday, 10.30am–4.30pm; Saturday and Sunday, noon–4pm. Admission free

Mission Santa Barbara

This is the most grand of the missions established by the Spanish and is often called 'The Queen of Missions'. Founded in 1786, it sits on a knoll high above the town and its design was based on the designs of Roman engineers dating back to AD27.

There is a small museum, and the gardens are particularly worth seeing.
2201 Laguna Street (tel: 805 682 4713) Open: weekdays, 9am–5pm, Sundays, 1pm–5pm. Admission charge

Stearns Wharf

The oldest pier on the West Coast is an extension of Santa Barbara's main street, State Street. It was built in 1872 and has the usual mixture of souvenir shops, restaurants and seafood stands.

At the end of the pier you will probably see the once-endangered brown pelicans trying to sneak fish from the anglers who seem to be a permanent fixture here.

SAN LUIS OBISPO

The fifth mission built by Junípero Serra is here, but its ruins are not of any particular interest.

San Luis Obispo is a college town. California Polytechnic State University, which has one of the finest agricultural faculties in the country, is based here.

There is not a great deal of interest to visitors but it provides a pleasant break on the drive up Highway 1.

SAN SIMEON

Forty miles north of San Luis Obispo, newspaper magnate William Randolph Hearst built what must be the most opulent and extravagant 'house' in California if not the nation.

Starting in 1919, Hearst Castle took 30 years to build at a cost of three million dollars. Today it is estimated that the building would cost 300 to 400 million dollars to complete.

There are 38 bedrooms, 14 sitting-rooms, two libraries, a kitchen and a theatre and that is just in the main house. There are two additional buildings that are guest houses.

The property is so big that four different tours are offered by the State Park Service who have administered the property since 1957.

It is the second biggest attraction in California, after Disneyland, with over a million visitors a year. Because of its popularity reservations are essential at the height of the season and are recommended at all times.

Each tour takes two hours, and for the first-time visitor Tour 1 is the best introduction. Wear comfortable shoes, there is a lot of walking to do!

To make reservations call toll-free 800 444 7275 within California or 619 452 1950 out of state. Open: daily, except for New Year's Day, Thanksgiving and Christmas. Admission charge

BIG SUR

Big Sur is specifically the name of a small town about 20 miles south of Carmel but it has come to be synonymous with a section of dramatic coastline that extends from the Carmel Highlands down to San Simeon.

The 90-mile drive clings precariously to the side of the Santa Lucia Mountains. It is a tortuous two-lane road that takes several hours to drive but the dramatic scenery more than justifies the journey.

Lookout points are provided all along the route and during the winter months give a bird's-eye view of the California grey whales on their annual migration to and from Mexico. The road passes four state parks and hundreds of square miles of wilderness spread east of Highway 1, and is penetrated by numerous hiking trails.

For many years this was a favourite hideaway for literary giants like Henry Miller and Hollywood stars Rita Hayworth and Orson Welles.

For information on accommodation and attractions contact: Big Sur Chamber of Commerce, Box 87, Big Sur, California 93920 (tel: 408 667 2156).

Land and sea meet at Point Lobos

POINT LOBOS STATE RESERVE

Robert Louis Stevenson wrote that Point Lobos was 'the most beautiful meeting of land and sea on earth'.

The Pacific Ocean constantly pounds the granite coast to create a bizarre and beautiful landscape capped by Monterey pines.

This 1,250-acre state park just south of Carmel is easily accessible by road, but the parking areas are small so in summer it pays to get there early.

Several trails exist in the park but for a short visit the Cypress Grove Trail should not be missed and will give a good introduction to this part of the coastline. Look out for the playful sea otters that frolic in the kelp forests off Point Lobos.

Trail maps and wildlife guides are available from the ranger station at the park entrance.

Point Lobos State Reserve (tel: 408 624 4909). Open: daily, 9am–5pm; in summer, until sunset.

CARMEL

This one-square-mile village by the sea is one of northern California's biggest tourist attractions.

Originally Carmel was a haven for artists and writers but they have long since been priced out of the market. The art galleries remain, however, all 70 of them! It is a town that is almost too perfect. There are no neon signs, no traffic-lights, no hoardings or bill-boards. There is no postal delivery. All 5,000 residents have to collect their mail from the post office. There are no house numbers or parking meters. There are even laws against eating in the street and wearing high heels. Needless to say, fast-food restaurants are not allowed.

This forced effort to remain 'quaint'

Peace and quiet at Carmel

attracts so many people during the summer, especially at weekends, that it is almost impossible to move. Parking in particular becomes extremely difficult.

There is no denying that Carmel does have considerable charm, but try to avoid weekends. It is a place to visit for ambience rather than sightseeing. The beach is particularly fine (see **Walks and Drives**), and so is the mission.

Mission San Carlos Borromeo del Carmelo

The Carmel Mission was the favourite of Father Junípero Serra who lies buried in the church. It was the second mission in the chain, built in 1771, and it remained Serra's headquarters until his death. It is located on a splendid site at the mouth of the Carmel River, overlooking the sea.

Extensive restoration has returned the mission to its original condition, and it is perhaps the most authentic and beautiful mission in the chain. The gardens are particularly fine.

3080 Rio Road, Carmel (tel: 408 624 3600). Open: Monday to Saturday, 9.30am–4.30pm; Sunday, 10.30am–4.30pm.

The exclusive residential and golfing community of Pebble Beach adjoins Carmel and can be reached from Ocean Avenue (see **Walks and Drives***).*

Fisherman's Wharf, Monterey

MONTEREY

In the early years of California, Monterey was the most important city. It was the Spanish capital of Alta California, then the Mexican capital in 1822 and the American capital in 1846.

After the discovery of gold the focus of the state moved north and Monterey became a major fishing port. Today it is tourism that keeps its economy afloat.

Cannery Row

(see also **Walks and Drives**)
John Steinbeck immortalised this street

of old fish canneries filled with eccentric characters. Gentrification has destroyed the old atmosphere and it is now just another tourist trap. The aquarium at the far end of the wharf is the one notable exception (see below).

Fisherman's Wharf

The wharf was built in 1846 as a pier for trading ships coming around Cape Horn. It was also used by sardine fishermen and whaling boats before the fishing industry hit the doldrums.

It has now gone the way of Cannery Row and is little more than a tourists' shopping and restaurant mall. There are, however, good views of the bay from the end of the wharf.

Monterey Bay Aquarium

(see also **Walks and Drives**)
The importance of this aquarium extends far beyond the Monterey peninsula. It is one of the finest and largest aquariums in the world with over 6,500 marine creatures on exhibition. *886 Cannery Row, Monterey (tel: 408 375 3333). Open: daily, 10am–6pm. Admission charge*

Monterey's Path of History

A dozen historic buildings are on the walking tour through the oldest parts of Monterey. Entrance tickets can be bought at any of the buildings, and the ticket gives admission to all of them.

The Custom House at 1 Custom House Plaza is the most logical place to start. It is across the road from Fisherman's Wharf and is the most important of the buildings. It is the oldest government office on the whole Pacific coast, and it was here that the US flag was first raised in 1846.
Maps of the self-guiding tour are available

JOHN STEINBECK

Most of Steinbeck's writings were based on Monterey or Salinas where he was born in 1902. Cannery Row in Monterey would probably have disappeared years ago had it not been immortalised in his classical novel of the same name.

Steinbeck attended Stanford University intermittently between 1919 and 1926 but never obtained a degree. To support himself, he worked as a labourer, and his experiences with the agricultural workers of Monterey County provided material for Tortilla Flat, his first novel to achieve popular success.

The Grapes of Wrath was published in 1937, and in the same year appeared as both a stage play and a film. The book won a Pulitzer Prize and established Steinbeck as a major American writer.

Several more books followed, including *Of Mice and Men, Cannery Row* and *East of Eden,* but none reached the critical success of his work in the 1930s. In spite of this, in 1962, he was the seventh American writer to receive the Nobel Prize for Literature.

After spending most of his life in California, he died in New York in 1968.

Solitude at Monterey Beach

variety of fish including tuna, swordfish, shark, squid, cod and salmon.

This is an ideal place to capture something of the flavour of the old Monterey of Steinbeck's time.

Pacific Grove
(see **Walks and Drives**)

Stevenson House
In California, it seems that wherever Robert Louis Stevenson spent a night has become a museum.

To be fair, he spent four months here in 1879 and the house at 530 Houston Street has been fully restored with 19th-century furnishings.
For details of opening times call: 408 649 7118. Admission charge

Salmon, not sardines, at Fisherman's Wharf

with ticket purchase. For opening times call: 408 649 7118.

Municipal Wharf
A small fishing fleet still uses this last working wharf in Monterey. Every day you can see boats unloading a wide

Missions

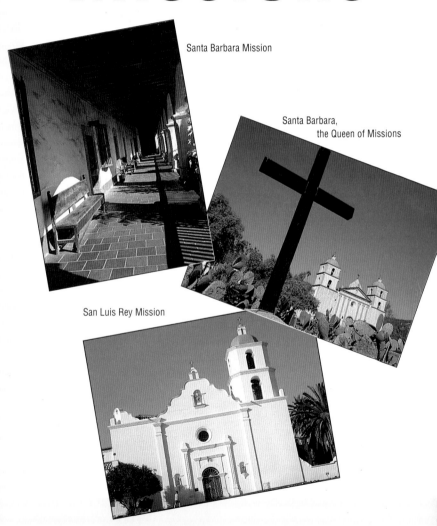

Santa Barbara Mission

Santa Barbara,
the Queen of Missions

San Luis Rey Mission

In 1769, when Father Junípero Serra was already 55, he travelled 750 miles by donkey, from Mexico to San Diego, to build the first of a series of missions that would eventually extend up the coast of California as far as Sonoma to the north of San Francisco.

Junípero Serra had moved to Mexico from his birthplace in Majorca when he was 37. He was a small man with a pronounced limp resulting from an injury in Mexico for which he refused to have treatment. At the time of his death in 1784 he had travelled thousands of miles and established a further nine missions in what were then the remote outposts of California. He is buried in the second mission he founded at Carmel.

Serra was succeeded by Fermín Francisco de Lasuén who, like Serra, had moved to Mexico in his 30s. He established an additional eight missions during his 18 years in the office of president of the missions, and he was already 66 years old when he started the project. It was de Lasuén who developed the style of architecture that has come to be known throughout California as the mission style.

The missions were linked by El Camino Real – the King's Highway. Streets bearing the same name, following the original route, can be found in most of California's coastal towns today. Highway 101 closely follows this route. All the missions are open to the public.

Carmel, Serra's favourite mission

San Buenaventura Mission, Ventura

San Francisco

*S*an Francisco is everyone's favourite city. Whenever a poll is taken, San Francisco invariably finishes in the top 10. Its visual appeal has a lot to do with this. It is built on a series of hills that not only help to create an interesting architectural environment, but also allow glimpses of either San Francisco Bay, the Golden Gate or the Pacific Ocean, as the city itself is surrounded on three sides by water.

This spectacular location on a peninsula adds further to San Francisco's charm. The city is small. It covers only 46 square miles and has a population of less than 800,000. The scale is human, and it is one of the few North American cities that is both pleasant and manageable to walk around.

The climate helps its reputation too. It rarely gets too hot and almost never freezes. Natural air-conditioning keeps the air clean and sparkling for most of the time. It does, however, get cold, particularly in the summer when the famous sea fogs roll in from the Pacific. Just because it is August in California does not mean it is hot in San Francisco.

Within two years of James Marshall discovering gold in the Sierra Nevada, San Francisco grew from a population of 900 to 25,000. Forty years later it was over 300,000.

This cosmopolitan population drawn by the lure of gold set the pattern for the future. It is an international community with a great deal of tolerance. Here is the largest Oriental population outside the Orient. A Chinatown bigger than many towns in China and large Japanese, Vietnamese and Filipino communities. Then there are the Mexicans. The Mission District is dominated by Spanish-speaking families from Mexico and Central America. You can spend a day there without hearing a word of English spoken. The Italians still have a very strong presence, although their traditional neighbourhood of North Beach is being invaded by Chinatown.

For well over a century San Francisco has retained its ethnic diversity, and its legendary tolerance has embraced the Beatniks of the 50s, the flower children of the 60s and now the largest gay population in the United States.

Many of these factors have led to an active and progressive cultural scene. The opera and symphony orchestra are both of international standing. Both legitimate and experimental theatre are thriving. Many of the great 20th-century artists such as Mark Rothko and Clyfford Still have made their home here.

Most long-time residents rarely think of earthquakes, although the 1989 Loma Prieta shock jolted many people out of their complacency. All modern buildings have to be built to very rigorous standards and are considered to be virtually earthquake-proof. Even many of the older building have withstood severe shocks, including the 1906 disaster. Fire has always been a bigger danger than the actual quake.

In spite of the 1906 earthquake and

several major fires, old San Francisco has remained remarkably well preserved. The old, painted Victorian houses have lost none of their charm even if they tend to be in some of the less desirable neighbourhoods. The cable cars still clank along as a living relic from the past, and Golden Gate Bridge commands the entrance to the bay as it has for the past 50 years.

People who have never visited California often speak of Los Angeles and San Francisco in the same breath. They could not be more dissimilar, whether geographically, culturally or politically.

Cable car terminus

CABLE CARS

The first cable car ran in San Francisco in 1873 and at one time there were 8 lines with over 110 miles of track. Today only 3 lines and 11 miles of track remain, but the cable car never loses its popularity.

The cable car does not have any form of power of its own. It moves by attaching a clamp to an endless moving cable below the tracks. To stop, the brakeman releases the clamp and applies the brakes. To move, he reattaches the clamp. At the end of the line the car must be turned around on a turntable and the passengers are often invited to lend some force to the task.

The quaint, clanking cars are as good a way to travel as any on San Francisco's congested streets, and the three operating lines cover several well-known tourist haunts. The Bay and Taylor cars leave Market Street, pass Chinatown and North Beach and finish at Fisherman's Wharf. Hyde and Beach cars also leave from Market Street, pass by Union Square, skirt around Chinatown, and travel on to Aquatic Park by Ghiradelli Square.

The California Street line runs from the foot of California Street by the Hyatt Regency Hotel, up Nob Hill and on to Van Ness Avenue.

During the summer be prepared for long queues. It is best to buy tickets before boarding and there are machines at the terminals and major stops.

To find out more about the history and workings of cable cars visit the Cable Car Barn on Mason Street. This is the main control centre, where you can see the actual cables running at precisely 9.5 mph over 14-foot pulleys called sheaves. There is also a good exhibit of old photographs, drawings and models, and some of the original cars built in 1873 by Andrew Hallidie. _Cable Car Barn, 1201 Mason Street, San Francisco (tel: 415 474 1887). Open: daily, 10am–6pm. Admission free_

ALCATRAZ

Until its closure in 1963 The Rock was home to some of America's most notorious criminals including Al Capone and, of course, the Birdman. It is now administered by the National Parks Service.

Most of the original cells, the hospital and dining-room are open and a self-guiding tour is available with a tape-recorded commentary by former inmates and guards. It takes about 1.5 hours. Both the ferry ride over and the tour are very inexpensive.

The trip out on the boat and the island itself can be very cold even if there is no fog, so take some warm clothing.

One of the most popular attractions in San Francisco, you should make your ferry bookings as far ahead as possible. *Ferries leave from Pier 41 next to Fisherman's Wharf starting at 9am, with the last boat leaving at 5pm in the summer and 3pm in the winter.*

Ferries to Alcatraz are operated by the Red and White Fleet from Pier 41, San Francisco (tel: 415 546 2810).

CALIFORNIA PALACE OF THE LEGION OF HONOR

This neo-classical building was built in 1924 by sugar millionaires, the Spreckels family, to honour the dead of World War I. They donated the building to the city and it now houses a collection of European art.

There is a fine collection of Rodin sculptures and in the entrance courtyard is one of the five original castings of Rodin's *The Thinker*.

Lincoln Park, near 34th Avenue and Clement Street (tel: 415 863 3330). The museum is undergoing a major renovation and will not be open to the public until 1994. Call for details.

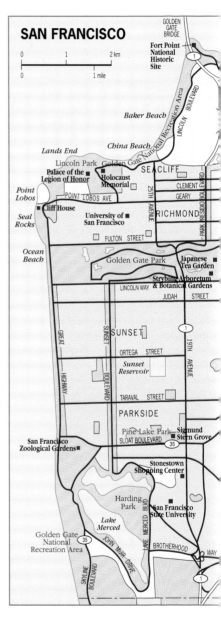

SAN FRANCISCO

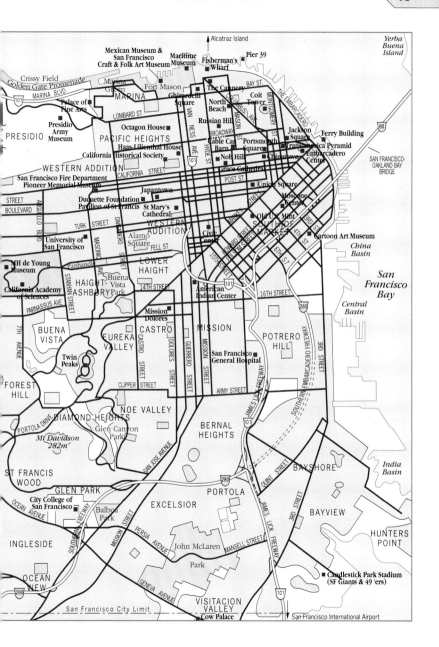

Chinatown

*T*his is the largest Chinese settlement outside Asia, and it is almost a city in its own right. The Chinese population in San Francisco is now over 150,000 and growing.

The Far East in the far west

Immigration started during the gold rush days when Chinese railway workers were brought over to construct the Transcontinental Railway. They were segregated into a ghetto which became known as Chinatown in the 1850s.

Today the Chinese population spreads way beyond the 24-city-block area of Chinatown and only a quarter of the city's Chinese population live there. However, Chinatown is still the true cultural and political focus of the community.

Grant Avenue forms the main street

and you enter through a gateway on Bush Street guarded by stone lions. It is the oldest street in the city and is always busy and congested, as you would expect for the most densely populated neighbourhood in San Francisco. Shops filled with cheap oriental souvenirs rub shoulders with restaurants, jade merchants, herb shops and fortune cookie factories.

To see the real Chinatown leave Grant Avenue and wander down some of the side streets, up on to **Stockton Street** and down to **Portsmouth Square**. The area is very safe and there is no need to be concerned by the oppressive crowds. Culturally, this is really a part of China. You will rarely hear English spoken and Caucasians stick out like sore thumbs. Chinatown is not a tourist theme park, it is the real thing.

To see where the Chinese shop, wander along Stockton Street any morning and join the shoppers hunting for the freshest exotic vegetables or maybe buying a live chicken from a stall on the street. Stroll through Portsmouth Square at any time of day and watch the old men playing mah-jong and chess. In the early morning this is a popular place to practice tai chi exercises.

All this exotic colour cries out to be photographed, but be careful. Many of the people here strongly dislike having their photograph taken and while you will not be in any physical danger, the verbal abuse can be awesome.

There are two small museums that can help put Chinatown into historical perspective:

The Chinese Historical Society of America
Documents the history of the Chinese in California. They claim to have the largest collection of Chinese American artefacts in the country.
650 Commercial Street, San Francisco (tel: 415 391 1188). Open: Wednesday to Sunday, noon–4pm. Admission free
The Chinese Cultural Center
Located on the third floor of the Chinatown Holiday Inn, there are regular exhibits of Chinese art and a few permanent cultural exhibits.
750 Kearny Street, San Francisco (tel: 415 986 1822). Open: Tuesday to Saturday,

10am–4pm. Admission free

A few temples remain that are worth a visit. The most important is the **Tien Hou Temple** on the top floor of 125 Waverly Street which dates back to the Gold Rush days.

The only way to experience Chinatown is on foot and lecturers from the Chinese Cultural Center lead a 1–2-hour **Chinese Heritage walking tour.** A culinary tour is also offered. Call 415 986 1822 for details and reservations. Several other walking tours are available. Check with the Visitor Information Center for details.

Bilingualism in San Francisco

CIVIC CENTER

City Hall is an impressive classical building with a dome even higher than the Capitol in Washington. Many of the buildings are government offices and not particularly interesting to visitors.

The buildings look imposing but the area has developed a seedy reputation. United Nations Plaza in front of City Hall is now a refuge for the homeless and the whole area has become a gathering place for panhandlers and alcoholics.

The History Room in the Main Public Library opposite City Hall has a good collection of documents, photographs and maps saved from the 1906 earthquake.

Across Van Ness Avenue from City Hall, still in a dubious neighbourhood,

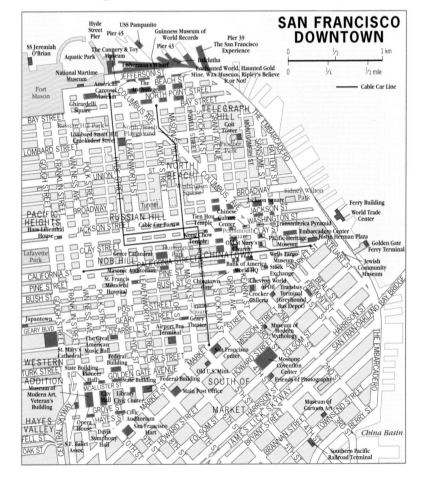

SAN FRANCISCO DOWNTOWN

0   ½   1 km

0   ¼   ½ mile

Cable Car Line

are three of the most important cultural centres of San Francisco.

Louise M Davies Symphony Hall

This ultra-modern glass and granite building has been the home of the San Francisco Symphony since 1980. Inside the hall is a 9,235-pipe organ, the largest concert hall organ in North America. Outside, a Henry Moore reclining figure complements the modern exterior.

Van Ness Avenue and Grove Street (tel: 415 552 8338). Tours are offered every half-hour on Mondays and Wednesdays, 10am–2.30pm. Admission charge

The War Memorial Opera House

The San Francisco Opera moved to this grand neo-classical building in 1923. The city has a tradition of fine opera and the great Enrico Caruso sang here the night before the 1906 earthquake.

The Opera House is shared with America's oldest professional ballet company, the San Francisco Ballet.

The opera season runs from September to December and the ballet from December to May.

Van Ness Avenue and Grove Street. Tours are offered every half-hour, 10am–2.30pm on Mondays only (tel: 415 552 8338 for details). Admission charge

San Francisco Museum of Modern Art

Twentieth-century art is the focus of the collection in the War Memorial Veterans Building, where there are works by virtually every important contemporary American and European artist. There is also an impressive archive of fine photographic prints, and photography exhibits are regularly on display.

The intimate **Herbst Theatre** is in the same building. The UN Charter was signed in the Veteran's Building in 1945.

In 1993 the Museum of Modern Art is moving to a new location in the Yerba Buena Center south of Market Street.

The Veteran's Building, Van Ness Avenue and McAllister Street (tel: 415 863 8800). Open: Tuesday to Friday, 10am–5pm, (Thursday, until 9pm); Saturday and Sunday, 11am–5pm. Admission charge

---

EARTHQUAKES

In October 1989, a massive earthquake, measuring 8.1 on the Richter Scale, shook many Californians out of their complacency. It was the worst disaster for San Francisco since the great earthquake and fire of 1906.

Eighty per cent of the population live on a series of fault lines that include the infamous San Andreas fault. This is the junction of the North American Continental Plate and the Pacific Plate which move past each other at the rate of about two inches a year. The movement is erratic and it is sudden releases of energy that result in earthquakes.

Earthquakes of varying magnitude are common throughout the state but they are usually too minor to feel, never mind cause damage.

The best place to see the San Andreas Fault is 30 miles north of San Francisco at Point Reyes. Here you can walk along the fault line on the Earthquake Trail and witness the magnitude of the 1906 disaster by the substantial displacement of fences crossing the fault.

Ecclesiastical Escapes

St Mary's
Cathedral

Grace Cathedral

St Mary's
Cathedral

Grace Cathedral

Building started on the great Gothic construction on Nob Hill in 1910, and it was not until 1964 that the cathedral was dedicated.

The main entrance doors are replicas of the Ghiberti 'Doors of Paradise' of the Baptistery in Florence. Inside, the morning sun casts a spectacular palette of colour across the cathedral as it passes through the many stained-glass windows. The east rose window depicts Saint Francis's Canticle of the Sun, and over 3,800 pieces of glass were used in its creation.

Grace is the third largest Episcopal cathedral in the country.
1051 Taylor Street, San Francisco (tel: 415 749 6303).
Open: daily, 7.30am–8pm.

Mission Dolores

Completed in 1791, this was the sixth of the twenty-one missions to be established by Father Junípero Serra. The adobe walls are four feet thick and the roof timbers are lashed together with rawhide strips. The 1906 earthquake made no impression on the building.

The price of construction was high – perhaps as many as 5,000 native Indians died building the mission from diseases caught from the Europeans. They are buried in a mass grave in the adjoining cemetery.
16th and Dolores Streets, San Francisco (tel: 415 621 8203).
Open: daily, 9am–4pm.

Old St Mary's Church

In the centre of Chinatown St Mary's sits incongruously among the restaurants and souvenir shops.

It has been a landmark since 1854, and was built mainly by Chinese labourers of granite from China and brick from New England which had to be shipped via Cape Horn.

Weekly classical concerts are held here.
660 California Street, San Francisco (tel: 415 986 4388).
Open: daily, 7am–6pm.

St Mary's Cathedral

This modern, white marble edifice is a remarkable architectural feat.

The enormous roof span is built without supporting columns so that views of San Francisco can be seen from all four sides. Stained-glass windows curve down and reflect on to 7,000 free-hanging polished aluminium rods of the baldachin.

This cathedral replaces the old St Mary's, destroyed by fire in 1962.
1111 Gough Street, San Francisco (tel: 415 567 2020).
Open: daily, 9am–5pm.

COIT TOWER

The tower was built as a memorial to volunteer firemen with a bequest from Lillie Hitchcock Coit, a 19th-century eccentric who chased fire engines. Popular opinion is that the tower was designed to look like the nozzle of a hose. This has never been verified.

The Pioneer Park car parking area below the tower gives good views of the bay. Even better, take a lift to the observation deck at the top of the tower.

Inside are 16 murals that are the work of 25 painters who created them as part of a make-work project during the 1930s depression. They are masterpieces of social realism depicting the lives of Californian labourers.

Telegraph Hill, San Francisco (tel: 415 362 8037). Open: daily, 10am–4.30 pm. Admission charge

THE FINANCIAL DISTRICT

As its name implies, this is the major commercial centre of San Francisco and the home of the Pacific Stock Exchange.

Business is the *raison d'être* for this area, with few attractions for tourists.

The TransAmerica Pyramid

This marks the heart of the Financial District. There is an observation area on the 27th floor that gives a good view of Coit Tower and North Beach.

Transamerica Pyramid, 600 Montgomery Street, San Francisco.
Open: weekdays only, 8am–4pm.

Pacific Stock Exchange

The Pacific Stock Exchange has two trading floors; tours are available but must be arranged in advance.

301 Pine Street, San Francisco (tel: 415 393 7969). Open: weekdays only, 6.30am–1.50pm.

Bank of America

The massive, black structure of the bank towers over most of the other buildings in the area. A bird's-eye view of the city can be had from the Carnelian Room restaurant and bar on the 52nd floor.

At the other end of the building, on the concourse, are two art galleries. Both show the work of noted local artists.

555 California Street, San Francisco (tel: 415 622 4997). Galleries are open daily.

The Embarcadero Center

The most distinctive group of buildings in the Financial District, they house a three-level shopping mall, offices and a couple of major hotels.

Parking in this area is extremely expensive and difficult to find, but there is usually space available in the underground car parking areas at the Embarcadero Center. Even better, with validation from one of the Center's shops, which could be as little as buying a coffee, you can park for up to three hours for less than the cost of a meter.

Banks dominate the district and both the Bank of Canton and Wells Fargo have interesting small museums.

The Wells Fargo History Museum

Full of memorabilia from the early days of the company including a restored, nine-passenger stagecoach, the main theme of the museum is the Gold Rush and Wells Fargo's participation.

420 Montgomery Street, San Francisco (tel: 415 396 2619). Open: weekdays, 9am–5pm. Admission free

The Pacific Heritage Museum of the Bank of Canton

This small museum focuses on the contributions that Pacific Rim immigrants have made to the state.

The building was the site of San Francisco's original Mint and it has been carefully restored, with a basement exhibit showing the original vaults of the Mint.

608 Commercial Street, San Francisco (tel: 415 399 1124). Open: Monday to Friday, 10am–4pm. Admission free

FISHERMAN'S WHARF

Native San Franciscans dismiss Fisherman's Wharf as one big tourist trap. They may be right, but if you can overlook the amusement arcade museums and the plethora of T-shirt and sea-shell jewellery shops there are still a few authentic corners.

A small fishing fleet still operates out of the harbour at the foot of Jones Street. Their catch is sold to the local restaurants, and at the junction of Jefferson and Taylor Streets old Italian families still operate crab stands selling freshly cooked Dungeness crab and sourdough bread.

For the old flavour of this part of town, walk along Pier 45 which is still a working wharf.

San Francisco Maritime National Historical Park

Just down the street is Hyde Street Pier which is part of the National Maritime Museum. Several historic ships are anchored here including the *Eureka,* an 1890 ferry-boat; the *Balclutha,* a Scottish merchant ship built in 1886 that rounded Cape Horn no less than 17 times; and a three-masted schooner, *C A Thayer,* that carried timber down the California coast.

2905 Hyde Street, San Francisco (tel: 415 556 6435). Open: daily, 9.30am–5.30pm (to 4.30pm in the winter). Admission charge

National Maritime Museum

The nearby National Maritime Museum has a display of model ships, photographs and various nautical memorabilia.

Beach and Polk streets, San Francisco (tel: 415 556 2904). Open: daily, 10am–5pm. Admission free

Both **The Cannery** and **Ghirardelli Square** are shopping complexes worthy of attention. Ghirardelli Square is the original home of Ghirardelli chocolate which is highly regarded in the US. You can still see the antique chocolate machines working, and even sample the goods. (See also **Shopping**.)

Ghirardelli Square, 900 North Point Street, San Francisco (tel: 415 775 5500).

GOLDEN GATE BRIDGE

The Golden Gate was named by John C Frémont in 1846 after the Golden Horn of Constantinople, three years before the Gold Rush. At 1.7 miles long, although it is over 50 years old, it is still one of the longest single-span suspension bridges in the world and one of the most beautiful.

Both a bicycle path and a footpath cross the bridge. The walk can get pretty cold, particularly if the fog rolls in, and remember you will have to walk back. There is no public transport to take you.

There is a vista point at the northern end of the bridge in Marin County and the view towards San Francisco is spectacular. Photographers may want to pass under the freeway and drive up to the Marin Headlands for the same dramatic view of the city but with the bridge in the foreground.

The Golden Gate Bridge is the most expensive toll bridge in the country, but the toll is only payable driving into San Francisco.

Golden Gate Park

*T*he 1,017 acres of parkland that stretch all the way across the western half of San Francisco can be credited to the work of 19th-century horticulturist John McLaren who turned these acres of rolling sand dunes into one of the great urban parks of the world.

This is a major recreation area for the local population. There is a boating lake, a lake for model boats, rhododendron dells, a casting pond for anglers and even a buffalo paddock and a working windmill. At weekends John F Kennedy Drive, the main road through the park, is closed to vehicles and opened to jugglers, roller-skaters, skateboarders and anyone else who needs open space and an enthusiastic audience. In addition to the scenic value of the area there are several major attractions.

Golden Gate Park

Asian Art Museum

This houses the collection of former International Olympic Committee president Avery Brundage. Nearly 12,000 oriental works of art spanning 6,000 years make up the collection, but only about 10 per cent of it is displayed at any one time. It is the largest collection of Asian art in the US.

There is a remarkable collection of Buddhist art from India, Tibet and Nepal; magnificent examples of Chinese lacquer-work and ebony carving and the largest collection of jade in the western hemisphere with over 1,200 pieces.

Entrance to the museum is through the M H de Young Memorial Museum, and one admission fee covers both. *Asian Art Museum (tel: 415 668 8921). Open: Wednesday to Sunday, 10am–5pm. Admission charge*

California Academy of Sciences

The Academy of Sciences is the oldest scientific institution in the west and has been located in Golden Gate Park since 1916. It is directly opposite the Asian Art Museum.

There are three separate departments within the Academy. The Natural History Museum has the usual dioramas of African and North American wildlife, a good mineralogical gallery and a major new exhibit on evolution.

The Steinhart Aquarium shares the same building, and in addition to a large collection of tropical fish there is a three-storey Fish Roundabout where you stand in the middle and the fish swim around ·you. There is also a dolphin pool.

The Morrison Planetarium is the third unit of the Academy. The usual astronomy presentations take place

during the day; in the evenings there are laser shows accompanied by the music of Pink Floyd and other rock bands.
California Academy of Sciences (tel: 415 750 7145). Open: daily, 10am–5pm. Admission charge

Conservatory of Flowers
This is the oldest building in the park. It was shipped over from London and erected on its present site in 1879. It is a replica of the great conservatory in London's Kew Gardens, and is filled with palms and other tropical plants.
Admission charge

Japanese Tea Garden
Adjacent to the Asian Art Museum the Japanese Tea Garden presents a world of calm and tranquility. It is laid out in a traditional Japanese style with curved bridges, waterfalls, stone lanterns and a pagoda.
Admission charge

The Dolphin Pool at the Academy of Sciences

M H de Young Memorial Museum
The 40 well-lit galleries of the museum house the most eclectic collection imaginable.

There is a good ethnographic exhibit displaying folk art from around the world. There are exhibits of period furniture, glassware, silver, and over 600 tribal rugs from central Asia. In addition to all this there are paintings from major European and American schools up to the turn of the century.

One entrance ticket also covers the Asian Art Museum and the Palace of the Legion of Honor.
Open: Wednesday to Sunday, 10am–5pm. Admission charge

Strybing Aboretum and Botanical Gardens
This is a 70-acre park within a park containing over 6,000 species of bushes and trees.

There is a Cape Province Garden with South African plants, a New World Cloud Forest and imaginative ideas such as a Biblical Garden where only plants mentioned in the Bible grow.

All the plants are labelled, and the avid horticulturist should be able to find plenty to fully occupy a half-day visit.
Admission charge

Marvellous Marin
A short ferry ride from San Francisco's Ferry Building takes you to one of the most spectacularly situated towns in the Bay Area.

Sausalito tumbles down a hillside to an almost Mediterranean corniche, giving unparalleled views of San Francisco.

This popular tourist destination has requisite restaurants, expensive shops and art galleries.

Haight-Ashbury, home of hippiedom

HAIGHT-ASHBURY

The name refers to the junction of Haight Street and Ashbury Street, which in the 1960s was to the hippies what North Beach was to the beatniks of the 1950s.

A few psychedelic relics remain. An occasional head shop still manages to stay in business; antique clothing stores rub shoulders with gay bars and art galleries. You may even see an occasional hippie complete with beads, kaftan and sandals.

JAPANTOWN

The area bounded by Geary and Post Streets and Laguna and Fillmore Streets has become the Japanese equivalent of Chinatown.

Unfortunately it has none of the colour and atmosphere of its Chinese counterpart. **The Japan Center**, a five-acre commercial development that is the heart of Japantown, is an ugly modern series of buildings that say nothing about Japan.

Once you enter the buildings things get better. Although the whole development is a little too bland, the shops do to some extent capture the flavour of Japan. The restaurants most certainly do. Many of the restaurants and sushi bars, both in the Japan Center and the surrounding streets, are totally authentic and serve excellent food.

The **Nihonmachi Mall** on Buchanan Street is one of the pleasant corners of Japantown. You pass under a *torii* gate to a cobblestone pathway that meanders past fountains. On either side of the mall are delightful little shops selling everything from shojii screens to antique kimonos. At the end of the mall, across Post Street, stands the five-tiered **Peace Pagoda** designed by the eminent Japanese architect Yoshiro Taniguchi.

LOMBARD STREET

The Crookedest Street in the World winds down from Hyde Street to Leavenworth Street in a series of hairpin bends.

There are spectacular views across to Coit Tower from the top before you plunge down the brick-paved street lined with carefully tended flower beds.

NOB HILL

On the high point of the California Street cable car line, Nob Hill still caters to the élite. This was where the wealthy of San Francisco built their mansions in the mid-1800s and in 1882 Robert Louis Stevenson described it as 'the hill of palaces'.

Most of these mansions were destroyed by fire following the 1906 earthquake but one survived. The imposing, brownstone mansion of James Flood still sits at the top of the hill and it is now the private Pacific Union Club.

Two of the city's grand hotels are neighbours of the Flood Mansion: the Fairmont, immortalised by the television series *Hotel*, and across the road, the Mark Hopkins.

Grace Cathedral sits on Taylor Street opposite the Flood Mansion.

NORTH BEACH

This is still a distinctively Italian neighbourhood in spite of recent encroachment by Chinatown.

In the 1950s it was the Bohemian centre of San Francisco. Jack Kerouac and other Beat generation poets would congregate in the Italian coffee bars and in the City Lights Bookstore. The bookstore is still in business on the corner of Columbus Avenue opposite Vesuvio's Bar, another Beatnik haunt, and it remains an important cultural gathering place.

Columbus Avenue is the main street through North Beach and it is crossed by Broadway, which has long had a reputation for its strip joints. A bronze plaque on the wall of the Condor commemorates the building as 'the birthplace of the world's first topless and bottomless entertainment'.

This tawdry strip of cheap sex shows is gradually changing for the better. Even the historic Condor has recently been converted to a pizza parlour.

North of Broadway, around Washington Square, life in Little Italy continues at the steady pace it has always known. Old men sit on benches in the square conversing in Italian and young men sit in the bars and coffee houses watching the world go by.

North Beach is a great place to relax and escape to Europe for a few hours.

Japan Center

The Old Mint, in use until quite recently as a branch of the US Mint

OLD MINT

The restored rooms of this imposing Greek Revival Federal building which opened in 1874 display the original furnishings of the Mint. The superintendent's office looks exactly as it did in 1897.

One very secure room has a pyramid of gold bars worth $5 million on display.

Other rooms have less valuable, but equally interesting, displays of western art, pioneer gold coins and one of the vaults, and a re-created miner's cabin.
5th and Mission streets, San Francisco (tel: 415 744 6830). Open: Tuesday to Saturday, 9am–1pm. Tours on Saturdays at 10 and 11.30am. Admission free

PALACE OF FINE ARTS

In 1915 the Panama–Pacific Exposition extended all the way across what is now the Marina District. Today there is only one remnant, the Palace of Fine Arts.

The building was designed by the eminent San Francisco architect Bernard Maybeck. It was originally a stucco construction that deteriorated so severely that in the 1960s the building was completely reconstructed from concrete.

The Palace sits by a small lake that is a permanent home to several families of swans and geese.

More than just a good-looking building, the Palace of Fine Arts houses an auditorium and one of the most fun museums in San Francisco.

The **Exploratorium** is a hands-on science museum for children of all ages. Over 600 exhibits wait to be discovered by visitors. *Scientific American* magazine deemed it to be 'the best science museum in the world'.

The Tactile Dome is one of the most popular exhibits in the museum. In this pitch-black sensory chamber, visitors have to feel their way through a maze of passages and textures in total darkness. It is so popular that reservations are required.
The Exploratorium, Marina Boulevard and Lyon Street (tel: 415 563 3200). Open: Summer, Wednesday to Sunday, 10am–5pm (Wednesdays to 9.30pm); Winter: Wednesday, 1pm–9.30pm; Thursday and Friday, 1pm–5pm; Saturday and Sunday, 10am–5pm. Admission charge. Free on Wednesdays after 6pm.

SAN FRANCISCO ZOO

Recent renovation has returned the zoo to its position as one of the top six in the US. The zoo was developed on an area

VICTORIAN HOUSES

Fine examples of Victorian architecture can be found all over San Francisco but the view from Alamo Square with the modern city in the background has become an icon of the city. Alamo Square is on Steiner and Fulton Streets and late afternoon is the best time to photograph this classic cliché.

On Franklin Street the Haas-Lilienthal House, which was built in 1886, is the only fully furnished Victorian house open to the public. The most unusual is the Octagon House on Gough Street at Union Street. This eight-sided house has been fully restored and tours are available.

Several Victorian houses have now been converted into bed and breakfast establishments.

of sand dunes out on Sloat Boulevard close to the Pacific Ocean. The collection includes snow leopards, white tigers, pygmy hippos and an excellent gorilla habitat. The new **Primate Discovery Center** has 16 endangered species of monkey.

Within the zoo is a separate Children's Zoo where all the animals can be both petted and fed.
Sloat Boulevard at 45th Avenue (tel: 415 661 4844). Open: daily, 10am–5pm. Admission charge

UNION SQUARE

If San Francisco has a centre, then this is it. The major department stores are here, and two of the grandest hotels.

The cable cars also go right past the square. The main theatres are around the corner on Geary Street and all the major airline offices are here.

Victorian elegance

Wine

When a Stag's Leap Wine Cellars' 1973 Cabernet Sauvignon won first place in a blind tasting in Paris, competing against the finest French wines, California wine had truly arrived.

The first grapevines were introduced to San Diego in 1769 by the Spanish missionaries. The vineyards extended northwards with the establishment of the missions, but it was not until the Gold Rush that wine-making came into its own. The Buena Vista Winery was founded in Sonoma in 1857 and over the next two decades European immigrants built wineries throughout Napa, Sonoma, Santa Clara and the central valley.

The industry ground to a halt during 13 years of prohibition and by 1933, when the law was repealed, the industry was in complete disarray.

Techniques and vine stocks improved over the ensuing years to such an extent that in the early 1970s California wines could compete with the best in the world.

The finest wines are produced from the white Chardonnay grape and the red Cabernet Sauvignon. However, very good wine is produced from virtually every variety of grape including Sauvignon Blanc, Pinot Noir, Chenin Blanc, Reisling, Merlot and California's very own Zinfandel – the Beaujolais of California.

The major wineries extend from Lake County and Mendocino down to the Santa Ynez valley near Santa Barbara. Napa Valley, a one-hour drive north of San Francisco, is the heart of California wine country and it is here that some of the world's finest wines are produced.

Many of the wineries offer tastings and tours. A guide to the California wineries is available from:
The Wine Institute, 165 Post Street, San Francisco, California 94108 (tel: 415 986 0878).

The crop at Pine Ridge Winery, Yountville

The Satui Winery, St Helena

Grape harvesting at St Helena

1988
ESTATE BOTTLED

STAG'S LEAP WINE CELLARS

S L V

NAPA VALLEY
CABERNET SAUVIGNON

Buena Vista

PRIVATE RESERVE

1988

CARNEROS

Chardonnay

ESTATE GROWN AND BOTTLED BY
BUENA VISTA WINERY, CARNEROS, SONOMA, CALIFORNIA, USA
Alcohol 13.5 % by Volume

Wine Country

*T*he wine country begins a mere one-hour drive to the north of San Francisco. Altogether four counties comprise the major wine growing area: Napa, Sonoma, Lake and Mendocino. However, it is Napa Valley that has become synonymous with wine and many of the finest wines in the world are grown and made here.

The Sonoma County wines are often the equal of their Napa neighbours and it was in the historic town of Sonoma that the California wine industry started in the mid-nineteenth century.

NAPA VALLEY

There are over 220 wineries in this valley, which is only 30 miles long and 3 miles wide.

Most wineries are concentrated along Highway 29 between Napa and Calistoga. Unfortunately, this road also has the greatest concentration of traffic. It is the main road through the valley and during the summer and at weekends it is so busy that the cars can be bumper to bumper all the way.

To avoid this, try the Silverado Trail that runs parallel to Highway 29 (see Walks and Drives).

Most of the wineries offer guided tours and tastings. Several wineries require advance reservations for tours and an increasing number are charging a nominal fee for tastings. The following producers are a few of the highlights.

The Wine Train, which runs from Napa to St Helena – one way to avoid the traffic jams on Highway 29

The Hess Collection Winery

At the southern end of the valley, close to the town of Napa, the Hess Collection not only has a self-guided tour of the winery but a multi-level art gallery with an impressive collection of modern paintings.
4411 Redwood Road, Napa
(tel: 707 253 2131).

Domaine Chandon

The tour here covers the manufacture of sparkling wine at one of the valley's few champagne-type wine producers. This modern winery also has one of the area's outstanding restaurants.
California Drive, Yountville
(tel: 707 944 2280).

Inglenook

The magnificent gothic winery was built in 1879 and is one of the most impressive in the valley. Apart from the usual tour, there is a museum tracing the history of the Napa wine industry from the 1800s and a wine library, with wine dating back to 1882.
1991 St Helena Highway, Rutherford
(tel: 707 967 3300).

Robert Mondavi Winery

Robert Mondavi has been one of the great innovators in the California wine industry. His collaboration with Baron Rothschild of Bordeaux developed a new breed of Californian wine. The tour of his efficient, modern facility covers the whole process of state-of-the-art wine making.
7801 St Helena Highway, Oakville
(tel: 707 963 9611).

Sterling Vineyards

A cable car transports visitors from the car park to the hilltop winery from which

Vineyards in Napa Valley

there are wonderful views of the valley.
1111 Dunaweal Lane, Calistoga
(tel: 707 942 5151).

Clos Pegase

This is one of the newest wineries and also one of the most interesting. The spectacular building was designed by eminent American architect Michael Graves who was the winner of a competition held in collaboration with the San Francisco Museum of Modern Art.

The winery houses the vast art collection of Jan Schrem, the owner.
1060 Dunaweal Lane, Calistoga
(tel: 707 942 4981).

Calistoga

At the northern end of the Napa Valley the small town of Calistoga has been an important spa since the mid-1800s.

The natural thermal activity in the area and the profusion of hot springs has resulted in a thriving business in steam baths, mud baths and massage.

Old Faithful of California

This is one of the few geysers in the world that erupts at regular intervals. If you have never seen a geyser, the novelty value may make this attraction worth the nominal entrance fee. A run-down group of buildings are an excuse for an entrance and prevent the geyser being seen from the road.

Behind these buildings is a scrappy piece of wasteland out of which a 100-foot jet of water shoots every 40 minutes. *Tubbs Lane, 1.5 miles north of Calistoga off Highway 29. Open: daily. Admission charge*

St Helena

This charming little town is the hub of Napa Valley and it still looks much the same as it did in the 1890s.

This is yet another place that Robert Louis Stevenson spent a few months in 1880 and the mandatory memorabilia collection is housed in the Silverado Museum wing of the public library. It was in St Helena that he wrote the book *The Silverado Squatters.*

Several wineries are close to town and the Beringer property to the north on Highway 29 is particularly interesting. Spring Mountain Vineyards at 2805 Spring Mountain Road, to the northwest of town, is a popular excursion mainly because of its role as the winery in the television series *Falcon Crest*.

VALLEY OF THE MOON

Only a thirty-minute drive west from Napa, the Valley of the Moon extends from Sonoma to Santa Rosa. This premium wine-growing region was named by writer Jack London who made his last home here.

Glen Ellen

The tiny village of Glen Ellen lies to the west of Sonoma on Highway 12 at the southern end of the Valley of the Moon. This sleepy corner of the wine country is notable as the home of writer Jack London.

Jack London State Park

One mile west of Glen Ellen is the 800-acre Jack London State Historic Park. The land was London's beloved Beauty

California's Old Faithful

ROBERT LOUIS STEVENSON

Stevenson was born in Edinburgh in 1850. In 1876 he met and fell in love with a married American woman, Fanny Osborne. She returned to California in 1878, much to the delight of Stevenson's parents, but the following year he decided to join her.

Stevenson was already suffering from severe respiratory problems when he reached California but he managed to eke out a meagre living in Monterey and San Francisco. In Monterey he used to walk along the coast by what is now Pebble Beach and it is thought that this provided material for his most famous book, *Treasure Island*.

In 1880 Stevenson married Fanny and they spent their honeymoon near St Helena in the Napa Valley. This resulted in the book, *The Silverado Squatters*.

The Stevensons returned to Scotland for a reconciliation with his parents before once more returning to San Francisco *en route* for the South Pacific. He died in Samoa in 1894.

Ranch and within the park lie the remains of The Wolf House, destroyed by a mysterious fire before completion in 1913.

After London's death in 1916, his wife Charmian built the House with Happy Walls, now a museum dedicated to London with memorabilia of his travels, particularly in the South Pacific. The park has numerous walking trails and is ideal for picnics.

Open: daily, from dawn to dusk. Admission free

Sonoma

The central plaza of Sonoma was laid out by General Vallejo in 1835 and it is surrounded by one of the finest groups of Mexican-era adobe buildings in northern California.

Just off the main plaza, the San Francisco de Solano mission is the most northern of the chain and was the last to be built in 1823.

The old railway depot at the spa town of Calistoga

Although Napa Valley now wears the wine-makers' crown, it was Sonoma where the industry started. In 1857 Agoston Haraszthy built the Buena Vista Winery at 18000 Old Winery Road, Sonoma *(tel: 707 938 1266)*. There are tours of the original caves and the grounds are a perfect spot for a summer picnic.

Buena Vista was the first commercial enterprise, but in 1825 padres from the mission planted a huge vineyard near Fourth Street East in Sonoma. In 1904 the Sebastiani family purchased it and they have been operating the winery ever since at *389 Fourth Street East, Sonoma (tel: 707 938 5532)*.

Mercer Caverns
at Murphys

Gold panning in
the American
River

The site of James Marshall's gold
discovery at Sutter's Mill

Gold

When James Marshall discovered gold in the millrace of a sawmill in Coloma in 1848, the course of Californian history changed dramatically.

Within a year, thousands of fortune seekers headed west and started the migration that continues even today.

Gold had always been the carrot dangling in front of the explorers of this frontier land, and once its discovery had been made towns mushroomed overnight.

The legacy of this period still survives in the string of towns along Highway 49 from Nevada City down to Mariposa.

'Weekend miners' still go panning in the rivers and some commercial mines have reopened. It is thought that as much gold again is still in the Californian ground.

Mine tours are given at the old Empire Mine in Grass Valley, and the North Star Mine has a museum with a vast display of mining equipment.

In the Malakoff Diggins State Historic Park, 16 miles north of Nevada City, you can see an impressive example of landscape erosion as a result of hydraulic mining.

A replica of Sutter's Mill, where gold was discovered, has been constructed on the original site in Coloma. Gold pans are available for rent for anyone wanting to attempt a re-creation of the historic event.

Many shops have California gold for sale and there is no shortage of museum exhibits. Perhaps the most impressive display of the immense wealth extracted from the California soil is the $5 million pyramid of gold bars on display at the Old Mint in San Francisco.

Samples of native gold

Sacramento

*R*ather than San Francisco or Los Angeles, Sacramento became California's capital city – and appropriately so, since the state's modern history began near here, at a site on the American River. Carpenter James Marshall, sent upstream to construct a new lumber-mill by John Sutter, one of Sacramento's first settlers, also discovered gold in the millrace. Sutter's dreams of an agricultural empire were dashed by the 1849 California Gold Rush and he died a broken and bitter man, as did Marshall. But almost overnight Sutter's small adobe enclave grew into a bustling commercial centre of well over half a million people. By 1854, Sacramento had become the state capital.

Sacramento is a city at once relaxed and refreshing – except in extreme summer heat when even rose bushes wilt. Most historic sights and other attractions are near downtown, easily accessible by car or public transport. At least one local event, the annual Dixieland Jazz Jubilee held over the Memorial Day weekend, is worthy of rescheduling one's holiday. Also worth doing are lunch or dinner cruises aboard paddle-wheel river boats. More ambitious water adventures include weekend delta cruises departing from (and returning to) San Francisco.

THE CALIFORNIA CAPITOL

The state's golden-domed Capitol building is Sacramento's stately centre-piece. Situated at 10th Street and the Capitol Mall (between L and N Streets). Particularly worth seeing are the separate Senate and Assembly chambers on the second floor, as well as the Capitol Museum in Room 124.

Outside is 40-acre Capitol Park, an impressive arboretum, and California's Vietnam Veterans Memorial. Free tickets for guided tours (offered daily in summer) are available at the museum office in the Capitol's basement *(tel: 916 324 0333 for information and to arrange group tours).*

THE CALIFORNIA STATE INDIAN MUSEUM AND SUTTER'S FORT

Near the Capitol, the California State Indian Museum offers a fine collection of Native American artefacts and exhibits which respectfully depict the material and spiritual development of California's first citizens whose various cultures have been almost obliterated by the state's subsequent history. Adjacent Sutter's Fort, the valley's first non-native settlement, represents that history. Established in 1839, even here only a few original adobe brick walls survived the raucous rampages of the Gold Rush. The restored fort complex re-creates civilised life in about 1846, and occasional Living History Days demonstrate settlers' survival skills.

California State Indian Museum, 2618 K Street, Sacramento (tel: 916 445 4209). Sutter's Fort, 2701 L Street (tel: 916 445 4422).

Both museums are open daily, 10am–5pm except major holidays. Admission free

THE CROCKER ART MUSEUM

Near Old Sacramento, the Crocker Art Museum is itself a work of art, in the high Italianate Victorian style. The Crocker is also one of the oldest public art museums in the west, noted for its California landscapes and photography. *216 O Street, Sacramento (tel: 916 449 5423). Open: Tuesday 1pm–9pm, Wednesday to Sunday 10am–5pm, and special hours for special events. Admission free*

THE GOVERNOR'S MANSION

Peculiar in California, and due to pugnacious state politics, is the fact that there is no official governor's residence – not since 1967 when then-Governor Ronald Reagan and family fled this fine old Victorian house, and it became an eclectic public museum. *16th and H Streets (tel: 916 445 6477). Open: daily except major holidays, 10am–5pm for guided tours only. Admission free*

OLD SACRAMENTO

At the west end of J Street, Old Sacramento is a colourful 'city' of refurbished buildings of the Gold Rush era and a state historic park in its entirety. Despite the freeway overhead, the ambience is authentic. Many of the commercial shops re-create Sacramento's frontier past as successfully as the superb museums.

The **California State Railroad Museum** at *111 I Street (tel: 916 448 4466)* features an exceptional collection of restored locomotives and unique old railroad cars, as well as history dioramas and exhibits. Outdoors, hands-on train enthusiasts enjoy the 40-minute ride on the Sacramento Southern Railroad, and special events such as the National Handcar Races held each September.

Also worthwhile in Old Sacramento is the **Sacramento History Center** at *101 I Street (tel: 916 449 2057)*, noted for its Gold Rush and multicultural history exhibits. The **B F Hastings Building** at 2nd and J, once the Wells Fargo building and the western end of the Pony Express, also houses (upstairs) the original chambers of the California Supreme Court. The **Big Four Building** at 2nd and Front, the original Central Pacific Railroad headquarters, includes (downstairs) a functional re-creation of the 1880s Huntington & Hopkins Hardware Store. The frame-and-canvas **Old Eagle Theatre** at *925 Front Street* offers live period theatre *(tel: 916 446 6761* for current schedule and reservations).

For almost-authentic fun, take a paddle-wheel river-boat ride aboard the *Matthew McKinley.* Choose either a one-hour tour or a lunch or dinner cruise; the boat departs from the L Street Landing *(tel: 916 441 6481 or toll-free 800 443 0263* for current schedule and reservations). Another river-boat option is the *River City Queen,* moored north of town *(tel: 916 921 1111).*

Old Sacramento if free, but museums and other attractions charge fees. Most public buildings are open daily, 10am–5pm. Free **Old Sacramento Walking Tours** leave from the train passenger station at Front and J Streets on Saturday and Sunday at 11.30am and 1.30pm *(tel: 916 322 3676).* For more information about Old sacramento, contact the Sacramento State Parks Docent Association office *(tel: 916 323 9278)* at the railroad museum or stop by the Old Sacramento Merchants Association booth at *917 Front Street (tel: 916 443 7815).*

Highway 49: Gold Country

*J*ust as Nevada is known as the Silver State, it is no accident that California became the Golden State. The 1849 California Gold Rush created modern-day California. And the Gold Rush began here, when James Marshall made the first gold discovery, on the western slope of the Sierra Nevada along the 300-mile stretch of small towns and rolling foothills now loosely connected by Highway 49.

The Spanish myth of *la veta madre* or 'the mother lode' refers to a single rich vein of ore once considered the source of all gold in the territory. Historical purists point out that the mother lode actually includes only the territory's southern mines, those from Placerville south. The northern mines include the areas of Auburn, Grass Valley, and Nevada City, as well as the wild and woolly Yuba and Feather River watersheds reaching to Oroville north of Sacramento.

A delightful destination for one-day and weekend excursions, California's Gold Country also warrants much slower exploration. The area's low-key attractions include historical museums and parks, boutique wineries and produce stands, hiking and cycling treks in some quite outstanding countryside, as well as gold panning, fishing, and (in non-drought years) superb white-water river rafting.

THE NORTHERN MINES

Auburn and Coloma
Partly included within the 240-acre Marshall Gold Discovery State Historic Park *(tel: 916 622 3470)* 10 miles south of Auburn, Coloma marks the spot where James Marshall found gold in early 1848. This birthplace of the state's Gold Rush, now a mecca for white water rafters on the American River's south fork, includes a replica of **Sutter's Mill**, restored historic buildings, an excellent museum, and commercial shops and galleries *(open: 10am–5pm daily)*.

The community of Auburn just north is noted for its historic Old Town and the Placer County Courthouse, built entirely of local materials and beautifully restored. Worth more time, though, is the Bernhard House Museum annex *(tel:*

916 889 4155), completely furnished with Victorian antiques.

Grass Valley
North of Auburn are the twin foothill towns of **Grass Valley** and **Nevada City**, popular getaways for Californians. Once home to notorious dancer Lola Montez, who scandalised Europe (and eventually even San Francisco), Grass Valley was also home town of Lotta Crabtree – Montez's protégé, the darling of the gold camps, and the first entertainer ever to become a millionaire.

Proud of its venerable **Holbrooke Hotel** and home-made Cornish-style pasties, a predilection passed on by hardrock miners from Cornwall, England, **Cousin Jacks**, Grass Valley's most striking attraction, is the mine they worked in. **Empire Mine State Park** at

10791 East Empire Street (tel: 916 273 8522) is a 784-acre indoor-outdoor museum of mine shafts and ruins, opulent buildings, gracious gardens, and interpretive walks and displays. The Empire Mine was one of the richest and oldest hardrock mines in the state when it closed in 1956. Owner Willian Bourn was one of the richest men in California; here, appreciate his family cottage.

Nevada City
Historically, Nevada City has been host to innovators and innovations. World-class soprano Emma Nevada and Andrew Hallidie, inventor of the cable car, were both born here. Nevada City created new and radical mining techniques, including hydraulic mining. Social engineering was also no surprise: US Senator A J Sargent, a local resident, prepared legislation which led to American women's suffrage. Meetings held here ultimately established both the University of California and Pacific Gas & Electric, the world's largest utility company.

Noted today for its fine Victorian homes, active arts community, and the historic **National Hotel**, Nevada City's most unusual legacy is actually outside town and quite remote. **Malakoff Diggins State Historic Park** *(tel: 916 265 2740)* is an oddly enchanting environmental horror, including a massive mine pit with colourfull crags and spires created by hydraulic mining in the 1870s. Malakoff also offers good hiking, camping, and the Gold Rush ghost town of North Bloomfield.

Beyond Malakoff Diggins, Highway 49 weaves through rugged Yuba River Canyon past the striking tin-roofed towns of **Downieville** and **Sierra City**, birthplace of the eccentric Gold Rush

fraternity of E Clampus Vitus. (The Clampers' ancient motto, 'I believe because it is absurd,' speaks truth even in modern-day California.) Beyond Sierra City is the **Gold Lakes** region and **Plumas-Eureka State Park** *(tel: 916 836 2380)*, where snowbound miners used mining trams as the world's first ski lifts.

The old gold town of Nevada City

Northern Mines Miscellany	
For more information contact: Auburn Area Visitors and Convention Bureau, 512 Ravine Road, Auburn, CA 95603 (tel: 916 885 5616 or toll-free 800 433 7575); Nevada City Chamber of Commerce, 132 Main	Street, Nevada City, CA 95959 (tel: 916 265 2692); or the Nevada County Chamber of Commerce, 248 Mail Street, Grass Valley, CA 95945 (tel: 916 273 4667; toll-free in California, 800 752 6222; toll-free from other states, 800 521 2075).

THE SOUTHERN MINES

Placerville to Jackson

South of Coloma is **Placerville** (also known as Hangtown, due to historic local enthusiasm for gallows justice). These days Placerville is primarily proud of its 60-acre **Gold Bug Mine** *(tel: 916 622 0832)* on Bedford Avenue just north of town, America's only city-owned gold mine.

First known as Pokerville, then Puckerville, these days **Plymouth** offers few pleasures except fine regional wineries, including **D'Agostini Winery** *(tel: toll-free 800 722 4849)* northeast of town on Shenandoah Road, the state's fourth-oldest winery and a state historic landmark.

Gold rush memories at Jamestown

The next stop south is **Drytown**, now mostly a collection of antique shops but once cherished by miners for its 27 saloons. **Jackson** is well worth several hours of exploration, with a side trip east up Highway 88 to both **Chaw'se Indian Grinding Rocks State Park** and the serene Gold Rush town of **Volcano.**

Angels Camp

Past Mokelumne Hill and San Andreas (where Gentleman Black Bart finally went to jail) is the little city of **Angels Camp** made famous by Mark Twain's first successful story, *The Celebrated Jumping Frog of Calaveras County.* The roads here were paved in 1928, the same year the community launched its annual Jumping Frog Jubilee (real frogs, rentals available) held in May at the frogtown fairgrounds south of town.

More interesting year-round, heading east on Highway 4, is **Murphys**, with its odd **Oldtimer's Museum** and the fine **Murphys Hotel** (genuine bullet holes in the doors, wonderful western bar). Nearby are **Mercer Caverns** and **Moaning Cavern** (see **Getting away from it all**). Up the highway is **Calaveras Big Trees State Park** *(tel: 209 795 2334)*, a few rare groves of Giant Sequoia in a pristine forest featuring good camping and hiking.

Columbia and Sonora

Columbia, the 'Gem of the Southern Mines' 10 miles south of Angels Camp, is a must-do destination for *aficionados* of American Westerns. Quite a few, including *High Noon,* were filmed here. The town's authenticity painstakingly preserved, Columbia State Historic Park *(PO Box 151, Columbia, CA 95310, tel: 209 532 4301)* offers entire city blocks of oddities – including the state's oldest barber shop – in addition to museums, an exquisite period hotel, saloons, stagecoach rides, and events such as the annual Firemen's Muster in May and June's Columbia Diggins living history weekend. The town is 'open' daily, 9am–5pm, and is a very popular family destination.

Adjacent **Sonora** has its own claims

to fame, including historic buildings, fine inns, and decent restaurants.

Jamestown

Just south is Jamestown or 'Jimtown', another picturesque city popular with Western film-makers. Downtown features antique and gift shops, plus the opportunity to practice panning for gold in the horse trough outside the livery stable on Main Street (free, for children only). But adults can also hunt for riches through **Gold Prospecting Expeditions** *(tel: 209 984 4653)*. Gold mining claims can be rented by the day.

Also fun for families is Railtown 1897 State Historic Park *(PO Box 1250 Jamestown, CA 95327, tel: 203 984 3953)*. This 23-acre park offers picnic grounds and an open-air collection of old railroad cars, plus tours of the old Sierra Railroad Company roundhouse (admission charge) and various steam-powered train tours.

Coulterville

Some 20 miles south is Coulterville, a refreshing rural community almost unperturbed by progress. A state historic landmark in its entirety Coulterville offers blocks of boarded-up buildings of the Gold Rush period.

Worth an indoor stroll is Coulterville's **Northern Mariposa County History Center** *(tel: 209 787 3015)*, a crumbling stone museum complete with rifles, gold scales, and Victorian memorabilia from *High Noon*. Across the highway is the impressive **Jeffrey Hotel** and adjacent **Magnolia Saloon**, complete with swing doors, musty memorabilia, and even a wooden Indian. The small park hosts community events like the annual Coyote Howl and Gunfighters, Rendezvous.

Bear Valley to Mariposa

From Coulterville, take the back roads route into Yosemite National Park (ask locally for directions) or dive down into Merced River Canyon on the loneliest, most treacherous stretch of Highway 49. The latter journey passes what remains of **Bear Valley**, one-time headquarters for the troubled mining empire of explorer John C Frémont, also California's first US senator.

Southernmost of the major gold camps is **Mariposa** ('butterfly' in Spanish). Just off Highway 140 at Jessie and 12th Streets is the **Mariposa County History Center** *(tel: 209 966 2924)*, an excellent free museum housed in the local library. The white-pine county courthouse on Bullion Street features the original floor and a good mineral collection. But the local crown jewels are out at the fairgrounds. The **California Mineral Exhibit** here includes very fine samples of the state's natural mineral wealth. For information, *tel: 209 742 ROCK.*

Southern Mines Miscellany

For more information, contact: El Dorado County Chamber of Commerce, 524 Main Street, Placerville, CA 95667 (tel: 916 621 5885); Amador County Chamber of Commerce, PO Box 596, Jackson, CA 95642 (tel: 209 223 0350); Calaveras County Visitors Bureau, PO Box 111, Angels Camp, CA 95222 (tel: 209 736 4444); Tuolumne County Visitors Bureau, PO Box 4020, Sonora, CA 95370 (tel: 209 948 INFO).

Lake Tahoe and vicinity

'*T*he fairest picture the whole affords', according to Mark Twain, Lake Tahoe in the Sierra Nevada is North America's largest alpine lake: 22 miles long and 12 miles across, with a 72-mile shoreline. But its size is not its biggest attraction. Its beauty is partially due to the incredible clarity of the cold lake water, almost as pure as distilled water. Peculiar is the fact that Lake Tahoe never freezes, due to the lake's great depth. Beloved by Californians, Tahoe's shoreline is largely privately owned. Travellers can enjoy the lake itself at popular public parks, however. The Tahoe area also offers some of the finest skiing in North America and trails into several spectacular Sierra Nevada wilderness areas. Near Tahoe are other fascinations, including the tiny town of Truckee, where Charlie Chaplin filmed *The Gold Rush*. Since Lake Tahoe straddles the California–Nevada state border, the garish glitter of Nevada's gambling casinos, particularly Reno and Carson City, the Nevada state capital, is also an attraction.

TAHOE AREA PARKS

Near Truckee just of I-80 north of Tahoe is **Donner Memorial State Park** *(tel: 916 587 3841)*, where an excellent museum and various artefacts tell the grisly tale of California's notorious Donner Party. A wagon train was trapped here in 1846–47 by winter snows and the pioneer survivors were eventually reduced to cannibalism.

North of Tahoe City on Highway 28 is **Burton Creek State Park**, good for forest hikes, in addition to (on the lake) small **Tahoe State Recreation Area**, popular for its beaches. In Tahoe City on West Lake Boulevard is **Gatekeeper's Museum State Park** *(tel: 916 583 4976)*, several acres with picnic areas surrounding a museum emphasising the area's native cultures

Tranquillity at Lake Tahoe

and natural history.

Centrepiece of **Sugar Pine Point State Park** south of Tahoe City is the 1903 **Ehrmann Mansion,** an elegant fortress built of fine wood and stone, part of San Francisco banker Isaias W Hellman's summer estate. The rocky lakeshore offers sunbathing and strolling. The park is also popular for picnicking and short treks, including a walk to the lake's only operational lighthouse.

Contiguous **D L Bliss** and **Emerald Bay State Parks** futher south are popular for camping, hiking, swimming, sunning, and boating. It is an ambitious shoreline trek from the beaches at D L Bliss to Emerald Bay. Shorter (at least on the way down) and well worth the effort is the one-mile Emerald Bay hike to **Vikingsholm,** a massive Scandinavian summer home built in the late 1920s at a cost of half-a-million dollars (tours are offered in summer). Another way to get to Vikingsholm and its fjord-like bay is by boat – a very big boat, a stern-wheeler, with tours departing from South Lake Tahoe *(tel: 916 541 3897);* dance cruises are also available.

Near the south shore beaches and Camp Richardson is the **Pope-Baldwin Recreation Area,** which includes the **Tallac Historic Site.** Here 19 historic summer homes (some fully restored) testified to Tahoe's past as the playground for California's rich and powerful. Exhibits in the **Tallac Museum** (inside Lucky Baldwin's Baldwin Estate) tell the story, or take a guided tour (summer only). Special events here include Sunday Chamber music, a bluegrass festival in August, and the weekend Starlight Jazz Festival (usually August into September).

Lake Tahoe was 'discovered'

internationally when the 1960 Winter Olympics were held at Squaw Valley, and it is still a world-class ski resort. (Some decades later, there are many others, some including facilities for night skiing and Nordic skiing.) Skiers and non-skiers alike still make the pilgrimage to **Squaw Valley,** even in the summer, just to take the tram for some breathtaking high-altitude views.

Tahoe Area Miscellany

For more information about the Tahoe area, contact: South Lake Tahoe Visitors Bureau, Inc, PO Box 17727, South Lake Tahoe, CA 95706 (tel: 916 544 5050; toll-free in California, 800 822 5922; toll-free from out of state, 800 824 5150); Tahoe North Visitors and Convention Bureau, PO Box 5578 (850 N. Lake Blvd.), Tahoe City, CA 95730 (tel: toll-free in California, 800 822 5959; toll-free from out of state 800 824 8557); and

Truckee-Donner Chamber of Commerce, PO Box 2757 (office inside the train station), Truckee, CA 95734 (tel: 916 587 2757). For parks information contact Sierra State Parks, PO Drawer D, Tanoma, CA 95733 (tel: 916 525 7232); The Tahoe Tallac Association, PO Box 1595, South Lake Tahoe, CA 95707 (tel: 916 544 6420); and US Forest Service Lake Tahoe, PO Box 8465, South Lake Tahoe, CA 95731 (tel: 916 537 2600).

The High Sierra

The Sierra Nevada is California's most impressive natural feature. This massive granite mountain range is approximately 450 miles long, starting in the north near Mount Lassen and ending in the desert near the Tehachapi Mountains, and 60 to 80 miles wide. Some 200 million years old, volcanic activity started its creation. The dramatic peaks and valleys of the Sierra Nevada, however, were jolted into position by earthquake faulting, and then sculpted and scoured smooth by relentless glaciers during the last million years.

Technically, the High Sierra refers to the 150-mile-long portion of peaks, highlands, and icy lakes above the treeline from north of Yosemite Valley south to Cottonwood Pass. In everyday usage, however, the term tends to include the entire range except the almost-urbanized areas of Lake Tahoe and Yosemite Valley. However the High Sierra is defined, its elegant elevations are most easily appreciated from the range's steep eastern ascent. Mount Whitney near Lone Pine, surrounded by similarly sized sister peaks, is the tallest mountain in the continental US (outside Alaska), reaching to 14,494 feet above sea level.

SOUTH FROM TAHOE

Highway 89 south from Tahoe leads into California's own big sky country, virtually inaccessible in winter except for highways serving major ski areas. Every sky-high highways pass across the Sierra Nevada has its attractions: wilderness access for backpacking, mountain lakes

Winter sports at Mammoth

and rivers, family campgrounds, isolated ski resorts and odd old hotels and lodges, vast dark forests and aspens fiery with autumn color.

The busy Highway 50 route to the valley over **Echo Pass** features some fine scenery, as does the one-time Pony Express route (Highway 88) west over **Carson Pass** and Highway 4 over **Ebbetts Pass**. Thrilling, however, is **Sonora Pass**: Highway 108 climbs to the summit in a single-lane switchback like a goat path then suddenly slides down the other side (no trailers or recreational vehicles).

Still more spectacular is Highway 395 along the eastern slope of the **Sierra Nevada**, reached from Tahoe via Highway 89. Along the way is minuscule **Markleeville** and its unusual Cutthroat Saloon. Just west of town is the worthwhile **Grover Hot Springs State Park** *(tel: 916 964 2248)*, quite popular for its public hot and cold spring-fed pools, open year-round except two weeks in September.

BODIE

The one-time gold mining boom town of Bodie is California's largest ghost town, an evocative and ramshackle collection of woodframe buildings now protected as a state historic park. North of Mono Lake and reached via Highways 395 and 270 (Bodie Road), Bodie is a must-see destination.

What remains of what was once one of the wildest mining camps in the West (famous for its wicked citizens, worse weather, wide streets, and bad whiskey) offers absolutely non-commercial witness to the desolation of frontier life. Preserved in a state of 'arrested decay', Bodie self-guided walking tours allow visitors to peer into the weathered

The pool at Hot Creek

homes, saloons, store, restaurants, and livery stables which populate this half-day's exploration. Bring water and a picnic lunch (no services available).

The town is 'open' 9am–7pm in summer, until 4pm the rest of the year (only the truly intrepid try to visit Bodie when the town is buried under winter snowdrifts).
Bodie State Historic Park, PO Box 515, Bridgeport, CA 93517 (tel: 619 647 644).

MAMMOTH LAKES

Noted primarily as a resort centre popular with southern California skiers, the Mammoth Lakes area also offers a respite from eastern Sierra Nevada sagebrush in the form of forests, hot springs, and geological oddities along area trails. Most famous here is Devil's Postpile, a fascinating collection of vertical basalt columns formed by slow-cooling lava flows. Officially 'not recommended' by the US Forest Service for swimming or soaking, Hot Creek is none the less an immensely popular public hot springs three miles off Highway 395 via Long Valley Airport Road.
Mammoth Lakes Visitor Information Center on Highway 203, PO Box 48, Mammoth Lakes, CA 93546 (tel: 619 934 2712). Open: daily, sunrise to sunset. Admission free

The limestone fingers of Mono Lake

MONO LAKE

Once known as the Dead Sea of California, million-year-old Mono Lake is a large alkaline inland sea on the high plateau east of Yosemite. Far from 'dead', however, Mono Lake is home during at least part of each year to over 300 bird species, including almost the entire breeding population of California gulls. The saline waters here make even the worst of swimmers almost unsinkable.

Most striking, though, are Mono Lake's vast, surrounding salt flats and unusual formation of tufa – freeform pillars of calcium carbonate (limestone) originally created underwater where calcium-rich fresh spring water flowed into the salty lake. These 200- to 900-year-old bone-white spires are now exposed to view, due to Los Angeles's thirst for new urban water sources. Since 1941, when Mono Lake's feeder streams were first tapped, the lake level has dropped more than 45 feet.

The best place to explore Mono Lake's tufa collection is the South Tufa Area off Highway 120. Nearby are some interesting volcanic formations including Mono Craters, Panum Crater, and Devil's Punchbowl. For more information contact the New Mono Lake Visitor Center in Lee Vining (tel: 619 647 6595).

SEQUOIA AND KINGS CANYON NATIONAL PARKS

Even when Yosemite National Park is as packed with people as a suburban shopping mall, Kings Canyon and Sequoia National Parks to the south are relatively unruffled. Contiguous and equal to each other in grandeur, Kings Canyon primarily pays homage to the High Sierra wilderness of Kings River country, while Sequoia shows off its stands of Giant Sequoia. Though Kings Canyon has big trees, accessible from campground trails, those at Sequoia's Giant Forest are incomparable. The everyday big tree measures 10–15 feet across and stands about 250 feet tall, but the giants are awesome indeed. The lowest limb of the 'General Sherman', for example, is 7 feet across and would create a canopy for a 12-storey building. *For more information about these two exceptional parks, everything from backcountry to natural history lessons (including wildflower hikes), winter snowshoe treks, and Nordic ski touring, contact Box E, Kings Canyon National*

Park, CA 93633 (tel: 209 335 2315) or
Sequoia National Park, Ash Mountain, PO
Box 10, Three Rivers, CA 93271 (tel: 209
565 3341).

The White Mountains

An all-day journey at best, a side-trip via
Highway 168 from Big Pine east to the
stark White Mountains and the
Bristlecone Pine Forest is worth the
effort. Here stand the most ancient living
things on earth, scattered groves of
gnarled *Pinus longaeva* or bristlecone
pine trees. Many of these sturdy, scruffy,
and seemingly dead trees are estimated
to be more than 4,000 years old. The
area is desolate, so start with a full tank
of petrol and bring your own water and
food (campgrounds available).
*White Mountains Ranger Station (US
Forest Service), 798 N Main Street,
Bishop, CA 93514 (tel: 619 873 4207).*

Mount Whitney and Vicinity

Not for solitude do visitors climb to the
top of Mount Whitney, highest peak in
the continental US outside Alaska.
During the mid-July to early October
snow-free season the 10-mile trail to the
top can become dangerously
overcrowded, so Forest Service permits
(available in Lone Pine) are required.

An interesting aside between the
mountain and the town are the
Alabama Hills, a dirt-road detour
through enormous granite boulders
perhaps familiar as backdrops for
Westerns such as *High Sierra, Bad Day
at Black Rock,* and *They Died With Their
Boots On.* More fascinating, though is
the fact that quite close to Mount
Whitney, via Highway 136 southeast
from Lone Pine, is **Death Valley
National Monument**, the lowest point
in the continental US.

Bristlecone pine

**High Sierra
Miscellany**

Local US Forest
Service outposts,
usually situated along
public highways, are
the most consistent
sources of
information for
remote areas of the
Sierra Nevada. Maps,
camping and
recreation
information, and fire
and wilderness
permits are available.
For further
information contract:
Alpine County
Chamber of
Commerce, PO Box
265, Markleeville, CA
96120 (tel: 916 694
2475); Bishop
Chamber of
Commerce, PO Box
690, N Main Street,
Bishop, CA 93514
(tel: 619 873 8405);
Lone Pine Chamber of
Commerce, PO Box
749 (126 S Main),
Lone Pine, CA 93545
(tel: 619 876 4444).

Trees

'General Sherman' is the largest living thing on earth. He weighs 1,385 tons, measures 103 feet around, 276 feet tall and is about 3,000 years old.

'General Sherman' is a Giant Sequoia. Sequoia National Park in the Sierra Nevada mountains is home to the big trees. The massive conifers that lived when dinosaurs roamed the earth only grow at high altitudes in the mountains of California. Apart from Sequoia, small groves can be seen in Yosemite National Park at Mariposa Grove and Tuolumne Grove and at Calaveras Big Trees State Park in the Gold Country.

By some botanical quirk, California is home for not only the biggest trees in the world but also the oldest and the tallest.

From Monterey to the Oregon border, giant redwoods live in a 30-mile-wide coastal fog belt. The tallest specimens, reaching heights of over 350 feet, and ages of up to 2,000 years, live in the far north near Eureka in Redwood National Park.

Groves of redwoods are never too far away on the northern California coast and an impressive group of trees lives within a 20-mile drive from San Francisco across the Golden Gate Bridge in Muir Woods near Mill Valley. The oldest trees are not much to look at and they grow in an inaccessible, hostile environment above 10,000 feet in the White Mountains to the east of Big Pine on Highway 395.

The road climbs up to a barren, windswept, rocky landscape scattered with gnarled, old trees that were growing when the Pyramids were being built in Egypt.

In the Schulman Grove of the Bristlecone Pine Forest, trees have been found that are over 4,600 years old.

Calaveras Big Trees
State Park

Redwood National
Park

Giant redwoods

Giant
Sequoia

Yosemite

*T*he High Sierra's crowning glory is without doubt glacier-scoured Yosemite National Park.

The Park was created in 1890 over an area of 1,165 square miles that includes the finest valley and high mountain scenery in the US, wildly picturesque with almost vertical walls of granite.

Its popularity is confirmed by over three million tourists who visit the park every year and create environment problems that are a continuing source of controversy.

The heart and soul of the Park is the *Yosemite Valley*. This 7-mile-long, one-mile-wide canyon attracts over 80 per cent of all visiting traffic, and in the summer it can be a nightmare. During peak holiday periods every single room and camp-site is booked not only in the park but also in the surrounding towns. Reservations are an absolute necessity at these times, and the earlier the better.

Paradoxically, car parking space is often available on peak holiday weekends. Local Californians are so used to the madding crowds visiting Yosemite throughout the year that they tend to stay away from the area when they expect the worst congestion.

The reason for all this popularity is apparent a soon as you drive past the entrance stations.

Most people enter Yosemite National Park on Highway 140 from Merced. This is both the shortest and fastest route from I-5 and the San Francisco Bay area. A more dramatic approach is by Highway 120 that eventually becomes the **Tioga Pass**, which at 9,945 feet is the highest vehicle pass in California. Most years heavy snow closes the pass from mid-October to early May.

Whichever way you enter Yosemite, you will eventually want to make your way to the valley. Few places in the world have such a concentration of natural spectacle. Sheer rock walls rise either side of the Merced River almost as soon as you enter the valley proper. Rising 3,000 feet above the valley floor, the giant granite bastion of **El Capitan** is reputedly the biggest monolith on Earth. As you drive directly below this massive rock face it is almost impossible to gauge the scale until the insect-like climbers come into view.

Skiing at Badger Pass, Yosemite

Several more imposing towers of rock loom above the 17-mile loop road through the valley including **Sentinal Dome, Cathedral Spires** and **The Three Brothers**. The climax of the valley is the distinctive silhouette of **Half Dome** that has become the symbol of he Yosemite Park and Curry Company.

Here in the core of the valley is North America's highest waterfall. The **Yosemite Falls** cascade 2,425 feet to join the Merced River.

In the midst of all this incomparable wilderness is a surprisingly extensive development of accommodation, shops and restaurants. Immediately below **Yosemite Falls** lies **Yosemite Village**. This is always the busiest place in the whole of Yosemite; the **Yosemite National Park Visitor Center** *(tel: 209 372 0299)* is here, where wilderness permits can be obtained for overnight camping trips. The area is a hikers' paradise and the centre has a good selection of guide books and trail maps.

The only privately-owned property in the park is the Ansel Adams Gallery located between the Visitor Center and the post office. They have an excellent inventory of fine arts and crafts together with books and photographs by some of the world's great photographers, including the legendary Ansel Adams.

Several places in the park give spectacular views. The classic vista is from **Tunnel View** on the road to the awe-inspiring **Mariposa Grove** of Giant Sequoia trees. The road past **Badger Pass**, California's oldest ski resort, leads to **Glacier Point** which, at 7,214 feet, gives spectacular views.

On the opposite side of the valley, the Tioga Pass Road crosses some of the most beautiful, unspoiled wilderness in

Granite walls rise sheer from the floor of Yosemite Valley

the state. **Tenaya Lake** sits at 8,149 feet surrounded by huge, polished granite domes. A little further along, the road opens out into **Tuolumne Meadows** before rising to the 9,941-foot Tioga Pass.

Yosemite Miscellany

One of the great classic hotels of California is the **Ahwahnee** (tel: 209 252 4848) near Yosemite Village. It is often booked for over a year in advance. The spectacular Ahwahnee Dining Room (tel: 209 372 1488) is like an enormous baronial hall with floor-to-ceiling windows overlooking the magnificent scenery of the valley. Jackets and ties are required for dinner.

On the road to Mariposa Grove, the **Wawona Hotel** (tel: 209 372 1488) is like a vision from the Deep South. A 9-hole golf course surrounds the white, colonnaded hotel building.

NORTH FROM TAHOE

LASSEN VOLCANIC NATIONAL PARK

Known to Native Americans as Fire Mountain, Broken Mountain, and Mountain-Ripped-Apart, Lassen Peak is the southernmost volcano of the Pacific northwest's vast Cascade Range. Just over an hour's drive east of the valley towns of Chico, Red Bluff, or Redding, Lassen Peak today is within a huge caldera formed by the collapse of its mother mountain (Mount Tehama) 30,000 years ago. Lassen is most famous, however, for its much more recent behaviour: surprise volcanic eruptions, culminating in a dramatic 1915 blast of steam and smoke which tossed five-ton boulders into the sky. Lassen's theatrics created such a thrill throughout America that this pugnacious peak and its breathtaking setting were protected as a national park in 1916.

Lassen Attractions and Treks

Unusual at Lassen is its easy access, at least during the few short months when the main road traversing the park (Highway 89) is unblocked by snow. Many of Lassen's most noted features are either visible or easily reached from the road, so families with small children and people with physical limitations can enjoy the wilderness.

Some treks are quite challenging, however, including the steep, well-graded switchback trail to **Lassen Peak** (start early in the morning; bring water and a sweater) and equally impressive **Brokeoff Mountain**. Some visitors try the park's 19-mile stretch of the **Pacific Crest Trail**. But for the truly intrepid backpacker, 75 per cent of this 106,000-acre park is preserved as wilderness.

Other Lassen Activities

Lassen Park is a volcanic wonderland, featuring three of the world's four types of volcanoes in addition to oddities such as boiling lakes, mudpots, and sulphurous steam plumes. The best place to appreciate Lassen's fiery modern-day presence, not to mention summer wildflowers along the way, is at **Bumpass Hell**, where the careless Mr Bumpass lost one of his legs to a boiling mudpot. (Such dangers still exist, so heed all warning signs.) Other fairly easy treks include **Paradise Meadows** and **Kings Creek Falls**.

During Lassen's regular 'season', usually form mid-June until October, park rangers offer free campfire talks as well as guided treks . In winter, snowshoe hikes and cross-country ski tours are offered.

Lassen Volcanic National Park, PO Box 100, Mineral, CA 96063 (tel: 916 595 4444).

MOUNT SHASTA

Shasta is California's mountain masterpiece, the state's sixth highest peak but more majestic than any other. Lassen's silent sister volcano, about an hour's drive north of Redding via I-5, Shasta stands alone, looming above the ancient lava landscapes and forests. Mount Shasta was one of Sierra Club founder John Muir's favourite places; he first climbed the peak in 1874. Indeed, the mountain's history is mostly one of mountaineering conquest, a feat possible today for any sensible person in reasonably good physical condition. On an average summer day, 100 or more people attempt the ascent to the summit; about half succeed. (Climbers must register with the Forest Service office in Mount Shasta City before and

El Capitan, Yosemite Valley

after the day's efforts.) There are few trails on the mountain, but other treks are enticing. And if Shasta's wilderness areas are too crowded, **Castle Crags State Park** about 20 miles south is usually sublime.

Mount Shasta City at the base of the mountain offers basic services, motels, and restaurants. For information about the mountain and town contact *Mount Shasta Ranger District, 204 W Alma Street (tel: 916 926 4865)*, and the *Mount Shasta Chamber of Commerce, PO Box 201, 300 Pine Street (tel: 916 926 4865)*, both in *Mount Shasta City, CA 96067*.

Halfway between Mount Shasta and Lassen Park via Highway 89 is McArthur–Burney Falls Memorial State Park. Teddy Roosevelt extravagantly called Burney Falls 'the Eighth Wonder of the World'. Nearby is very remote Ahjumawi Lava Springs State Park, reachable only by boat, home to nesting waterfowl and bald eagles. (For information on both, *tel: 916 335 2777*).

Winter Recreation

Not famous as a ski resort, Lassen National Park still offers both challenging and family-friendly downhill ski slopes. Almost better, though, are the park's Nordic trails and ranger-guided snowshoe hikes. For more information, contact park headquarters or Lassen Park Ski Area, 2150 Main Street, Suite 7, Red Bluff, CA 96080 (tel: 916 595 3376). For Mount Shasta winter sports information, contact the Chamber of Commerce, the ranger district, the Castle Lake Nordic Ski Center, PO Box 660, Mt Shasta, CA 96067 (tel: 916 926 5382), and Mount Shasta Ski Park, 104 Siskiyou Avenue, Mt Shasta, CA 96067 (tel: 916 926 3174 or 926 5254).

The North Coast

Zigzagging north to the Oregon border from San Francisco's Golden Gate, the remote north coast is perhaps California's greatest treasure. Rolling headlands are common close to San Francisco. But further north the shoreline becomes rugged and rocky, in stark contrast to gentle coastal foothills, and there are great foggy stands of rare coastal redwoods, the tallest trees on earth along with varied wildlife.

GOLDEN GATE NATIONAL RECREATION AREA

Though the Golden Gate Bridge and a small coastal strip in San Francisco is included, Golden Gate National Recreation Area (GGNRA) primarily includes the **Marin Headlands** and vast open spaces stretching north to Olema, bordering Point Reyes. Dramatic seacliffs, rolling hills, and protected ocean-facing valleys are temptations for serious trekkers.

GGNRA also includes the **Point Bonita Lighthouse**, several former US military installations, the **Marine Mammal Center** (a volunteer-staffed

Drake's Bay, Point Reyes, the possible site of Drake's landing in 1579

marine wildlife hospital), and the **Marin Headlands Visitor Center**, noted for its science and other educational exhibits. Quite unique and endlessly popular for tours is **Alcatraz Island**, one of America's most famous prisons (see page 92). *Visitor centres are open daily, 8.30am–4.30pm. For more information, contact Golden Gate National Recreational Area, Building 201, Fort Mason, San Francisco, CA 94123 (tel: 415 556 0560). For Alcatraz tour reservations, tel: 415 546 2805.*

WEST MARIN PARKS

Surrounded by the vast acreage of the Golden Gate National Recreational Area are other public and private parks, most of these easily reached from Highway 1. Well known for its fine mountaintop views is **Mount Tamalpais State Park,** which includes **Muir Woods** – an unmissable destination for redwood sightseers.

North of Stinson Beach near serene Bolinas Lagoon is **Audubon Canyon Ranch,** a safe haven for many bird species and a rookery for egrets and great blue herons (nesting sites visible during the March-July nesting season). East of Point Reyes via Sir Francis Drake Boulevard is **Samuel P Taylor State Park,** redwoods and mixed forests with extensive trails and a paved bicycle path. Scattered in sections north of Point Reyes Station and Inverness is **Tomales Bay State Park,** where the sunny and protected inland beaches are the main attraction.

POINT REYES NATIONAL MONUMENT

Popular in winter for whale-watching these 65,000 acres of dazzling beaches, coastal dunes, lagoons, marshes, and hilltop forests at Point Reyes National Monument in Marin County are perfect for outdoor excursions almost any time of year. Hiking trails extend in all directions; short trails from the **Bear Valley Visitor Center** lead to the US Park Service's **Morgan Horse Ranch** and **Kule Loklo,** a re-creation of a typical local Native American community.

The truly imaginative might seek evidence of privateer Sir Francis Drake, after whom the estuary here is named. Historians agree that Drake came ashore

More on Marin Parks

For more information on the area's smaller parks, contact Muir Woods National Monument, Mill Valley, CA 94941 (tel: 415 388 2595); Mount Tamalpais State Park, 801 Panoramic Highway, Mill Valley, CA 94941 (tel: 415 388 2070; 383 0155 for theatre schedule); Audubon Canyon Ranch, 4900 Shoreline Highway, Stinson Beach, CA 94970 (tel: 415 383 1644); Samuel P Taylor State Park, PO Box 251, Lagunitas, CA 94952 (tel: 415-488 9897); and Tomales Bay State Park, Star Route, Inverness, CA 94937 (tel: 415 669 1140).

at 'a fit and convenient harbour' somewhere in California in June 1579. People still search for signs of Drake's treasure, which some believe he jettisoned.

It is a short but many-stepped trip to the **Point Reyes Lighthouse,** known for its astounding views. On a clear day (when the fog lifts), look due south to see the Farallon Islands, a UNESCO Biosphere Reserve and the largest rookery for a great variety of seabirds south of Alaska.

Also worth a stop, on the way to the Palomarin Trailhead, is the **Point Reyes Bird Observatory** *(tel: 415 868 0655),* the first such facility in the US when it was established in 1965.

For information, including a current schedule of year-round classes and field seminars, stop by any of the monument's three visitor centres or contact *Point Reyes National Seashore, Point Reyes CA 94956 (tel: 415 663 1092).*

THE SONOMA COAST

'Spectacular' is the scenic synonym for the Highway 1 tour of the Sonoma County coast. Apparently Alfred Hitchcock agreed, since he chose the coastal village of Bodega Bay to film *The Birds*. Aside from spotting Hitchcock settings, today the area is popular for beachcombing, whale-watching, and eating seafood (including local Dungeness crab).

From Bodega Bay north to Jenner are the collected **Sonoma Coast State Beaches**, where the dark and dramatic face of the coast starts to show itself. (Most of the area is not recommended for swimming, and caution is advisable even for tame activities like tidepool exploration. Offshore eddies, undertows, riptides and rogue waves are common.) North of Jenner and the Russian River is reconstructed **Fort Ross State Historic Park** *(open: daily, 10am–4.30pm, tel: 707 847 3286)*, established in 1812 as imperial Russia's most distant outpost. Further north, **Salt Point State Park** and **Kruse Rhododendron Preserve** *(tel: 707 847 3221 for both)* offer more natural attractions in any season (particularly during peak bloom in April or May).

MENDOCINO, FORT BRAGG, AND VICINITY

The entire town of Mendocino, a tiny woodframe village known for its Cape Cod architecture, is included on the National Register of Historic Places. (To get oriented, start at the Ford House interpretive centre on Main and take the walking tour. See **Walks and Drives**.) Once a lumber 'dog-hole port' and more recently an artists' enclave, modern-day Mendocino has become a north-coast tourist mecca with abundant small shops.

More fascinating is exploring the area's small state parks, starting with **Mendocino Headlands**. For more information, contact *Mendocino Area State Parks, PO Box 440, Mendocino, CA 95460 (tel: 707 937 5804)*. Nearby is working-class **Fort Bragg**, a small city noted for its botanical gardens, the fine fresh seafood 'off the boat' at Noyo Harbor, and the Skunk Train ride to Willits.

For more information, contact the *Fort Bragg-Mendocino Coast Chamber of Commerce, PO Box 1141 (332 N Main Street) Fort Bragg, CA 95437 (tel: 707 964 3153), open most weekdays, 9am–5pm; Saturday, 11am–4pm.*

South of Mendocino then inland via Highway 128 is the fascinating **Anderson Valley** area, a surviving farming area centred on Boonville. The area is noted for its almost-lost local dialect of Bootling, its Buckhorn Saloon brewpub, and the **Mendocino County Fair and Apple Show** (one of the last non-commercial county fairs remaining in America).

THE LOST COAST

The wild coast north of Mendocino eventually becomes so rugged that the Coast Highway avoids it and veers inland to join Highway 101. For the truly adventurous, California's 'Lost Coast' is accessible via various narrow roads and routes starting from Garberville-Redway, Humboldt Redwoods, and Ferndale. For information, stop by state park headquarters at **Humboldt Redwoods** or contact **Sinkyone Wilderness**, *PO Box 245, Whitethorn, CA 95989 (tel: 707 986 7711)*.

THE REDWOOD PARKS

The north coast's finest feature, its virgin

groves of *Sequoia sempervirens* or coastal redwoods, are best appreciated in Humboldt and Del Norte counties.

Hugging Highway 101 just north of Garberville and Redway is **Humboldt Redwoods State Park**, a fine preserve with 50,000 acres of almost unvisited redwood groves and upland grasslands brushed with mixed conifers and oaks. There are traditional tourist attractions too, especially along the old highway's **Avenue of the Giants**. Most notable, in Meyer Flat, is the **Shrine Drive-Thru-Tree**, one of the state's oldest tourist attractions (wagon trains once drove through it).

Further north, beyond the fascinations of the small Victorian village of **Ferndale** and the attractions of adjacent **Eureka** and **Arcata**, are almost unseen treasures. **Redwood National Park**, which now incorporates three exceptional state parks, protects most of what remains of California's original two million acres of virgin coastal redwoods (plus much over-logged acreage). Home

Flowers in profusion at Humboldt Bay

to three of the world's six largest trees (including the tallest, 368-foot 'Howard Libby' Redwood), over 1,000 species of animal and plant life thrive here including rare Roosevelt elk and (off shore, in season) California gray whales.

Redwood Miscellany

For more information, contact Humboldt Redwood State Park PO Box 100, Weott, CA 95571 (tel: 707 946 2311) and Redwood National Park, Orick Information Center, PO Box 234, Orick, CA 95555 (tel: 707 488 2171).

Information about Prairie Creek, Del Norte Coast, and Jedediah Smith redwoods state parks, all included within the national park, is also provided by the Orick Center.

Getting Away From it All

ANGEL ISLAND

This is the largest island in San Francisco Bay and can easily be seen to the left of Alcatraz.

Angel Island is covered with forest, and herds of deer roam free. It was the Ellis Island of the west, used as a quarantine station for Asian immigrants. During World War II it was used as an internment camp for Japanese Americans, and the old buildings have been converted into a museum.

Visit the island for picnics, bicycling and hiking. The hike around the island is six miles long and from the top there are 360-degree views of the Bay Area. No motor vehicles are allowed on the island. Access is by ferry from Pier 41 in San Francisco. It operates daily in the summer and at weekends during winter. *Red and White Fleet, Pier 41, San Francisco (tel: 415 546 2810).*

BALLOONING: Hot Air and Breathtaking Scenery

Hot air ballooning is a popular diversion in various California locales, perhaps most notably in Napa Valley. One company, the oldest wine country ballooning firm, offers dawn launches from Domaine Chandon followed by brunch with sparkling wines. For information: **Napa Valley Balloons, Inc**, *PO Box 2860, Yountville, CA 94599 (tel: 707 253 2224, or toll-free in California 800 253 2224).*

For an unusual variation on the theme, consider 'white-water ballooning' or the 'splash-and-dash' approach – a Gold Country experience down, along, and sometimes in the American River's south fork. Since pilot Alan Ehrgott and wife Cindi own a bed and breakfast inn the bed, breakfast, and balloon package is a bargain. For information: **Coloma Country Inn**, *PO Box 502, Coloma, CA 95613 (tel: 916 622 6919).*

In southern California, the high desert around Temecula is quite popular for high-flying balloonists.

Environment-friendly tours at Mammoth

BICYCLE 'SKIING' AND TOURS

In summer, Alpine ski enthusiasts can schuss down the slopes on mountain bikes, a popular new pastime now that many resorts are exploring year-round recreation options. Mammoth Mountain on the Sierra Nevada's eastern slope offers 60 miles of ski runs 'groomed' in summer for cycle touring. Guided bike tours, which start from the Mammoth Mountain Inn, include destinations such as Devil's Postpile and Rainbow Falls as well as Mono Lake and the ghost town of Bodie. *For information: Mammoth Mountain Bike Park or Mammoth Adventure Connection, tel: 619 934 0606 for both.*

Tamer is the Sonoma Valley Tour de Vins, a 15-mile trek which offers winery stops and a taste of local history.

For information: Wheel Escapes, 100 Magnolia Avenue, Larkspur, CA 94939 (tel: 415 461 6903).

A bird's-eye view of the countryside from the silent confines of a hot-air balloon, here floating majestically over the Napa Valley vineyards

THE BLUE GOOSE MURDER MYSTERY

The small steam-powered Blue Goose excursion train in the town of Yreka north of Mount Shasta offers seasonal family fun – and a very special summer adventure. An annual summer fund-raising benefit, the day-long Murder on the Blue Goose Express mystery tour, includes train fare, two meals, even a party afterwards. Participants each receive a 'script' for their part in the drama and are expected to wear period attire. Advance planning is mandatory. *For information: Yreka Western Railroad, PO Box 660, Yreka, Ca 96097 (tel: 916 842 4146).*

FABULOUS FILOLI

Woodside is a rural oasis on the San Francisco peninsula. This exclusive community close to Stanford is home to one of the great 'stately' homes of California.

The 43-room mansion at Filoli was designed by Willis Polk in 1916 and, although the house is well worth a visit, it is the 16 acres of themed formal enclosed gardens that are the main attraction. Eighteen gardeners were required for their maintenance and none of their former glory has disappeared. Reservations are required for tours – call *415 364 2880.*

FARM FESTIVALS

Unusual and sometimes highly entertaining in California are the multitude of community farm festivals which have sprouted up over the years. Most famous, perhaps, is the annual Gilroy Garlic Festival south of San Jose, where 150,000-plus people descend to celebrate the stinking rose with samples of garlic perfume and all-you-can-eat garlic ice cream (a few gallons usually feed the entire crowd) as well as big bands and other entertainment.

Other regional festivals include the Artichoke Festival in Castroville, Old Sacramento's Tomato Festival and Garden Bazaar, the Great Monterey Squid Festival, the Brussels Sprouts Festival in Santa Cruz, the Stockton Asparagus Festival, and Watsonville's Strawberry Festival. Even more obscure are events such as Yuba City's Prune Festival, the Colusa Rice and Waterfowl Festival, the Pear Fair in Courtland, and Isleton's Crawdad Festival. California also offers an endless array of ethnic events.

For a current events calendar, a listing of ethnic events, and to request a listing of local chambers of commerce (best sources for obscure events information), contact the **California Office of Tourism**, *1121 L Street, Suite 103, Sacramento, California 95814 (tel: 916 322 1396).*

KAYAKING: Silent Nature Tours

Perhaps most unobtrusive of all nature touring options is silently gliding on the water. Kayaking is the latest California craze. It takes skill, but even novices can learn enough in a lesson or two to manage most day-long outings (depending on weather conditions). For information: **Blue Water Ocean Kayak**

Tours (trips including Bolinas at Point Reyes, China Camp, and Mendocino), *PO Box 1003, Fairfax, CA 94930 (tel: 415 456 8956);* **Kayak Tahoe**, *PO Box 11129, Tahoe Paradise, CA 95708 (tel: 916 544 2011;* **Monterey Bay Kayaks**, *693 Del Monte Avenue, Monterey, CA 93940 (tel: 408 373 5357, or toll-free in California, 800 649 kelp);* **Sea Trek** (trips to Angel Island, Bolinas Lagoon, Drake's Estero, even moonlight dinner runs to Sam's in Tiburon), *85 Liberty Ship Way, Schoonmaker Point, Sausalito, CA 94965 (tel: 415 332 4457).*

MAMAS AND LLAMAS ON THE TRAIL

With these unusual beasts of burden carrying most of the load, a llama trip into the Sierra Nevada is an unforgettable experience. One company specialises in environmental education along the trail, hiring university professors and other experts as guides. For information: **Mama's Llamas**, *PO Box 665, El Dorado, CA 95623 (tel: 916 622 2566).* Other Sierra Nevada packers and guides, using horses in summer only, operate from eastern slope trailheads. For a complete listing of reputable firms contact **Eastern High Sierra Packers Association**, *Bishop Chamber of Commerce, 690 N. Main Street, Bishop, CA 93514 (tel: 619 873 8405).*

MONO LAKE AND ENVIRONMENTAL EDUCATION

The Mono Lake Committee – environmental activists who battle, in the courts and through the media, with Los Angeles Water and Power over the future of the lake's watershed – offers an excellent array of field seminars (from naturalist-led bird and biology tours to weekend study excursions) and classes in photography, Paiute basket-making and more. For information: **Mono Lake Committee**, *PO Box 29, Lee Vining, CA 93541 (tel: 619 647 6386)*.

Other reputable sources for outdoor experiences with an environment-conscious slant include the **University of California's California Adventures**, *2301 Bancroft Avenue, Berkeley, CA 94720 (tel: 415 642 4000)* and the **Yosemite Association**, *P O Box 545, Yosemite National Park, CA 95389 (tel: 209 372 4714)*.

RIDING A SKUNK IN THE DAYLIGHT

The Skunk Train Tour from Fort Bragg to Willits is a north coast tradition, harking back to the area's lumbering heyday. The full 40-mile route offers cliff-hanging scenery and sky-high trestle travel through the Noyo River Gulch. The old steam Super Skunk engine chugs out only on Saturday half-day runs; a diesel engine pulls the load on longer and summer outings. On full-day trips, it is also possible to start and end in Willits. For more information: **California Western Railroad**, *P O Box 907, Fort Bragg, CA 95437 (tel: 707 964 6371)*.

After appreciating the Willits Station, an architectural work of art crafted from clear heart redwood, adventurous rail travellers can roll north from Willits to Eureka on the north coast.

This is the most spectacular railroad route in California side-winding through the wild Eel River Canyon slowly enough to watch wildlife, sliding through Scotia and across the Scotia Bluffs, then slipping past the coastal plains farmland to Humboldt Bay. One-way and round trips are available, usually scheduled from late May through to October. For information: **Redwood Coast Railroad Company**, *293 E. Commercial Street, Willits, CA 95490 (tel: toll-free 800 482 7100 in California)*.

This says it all!

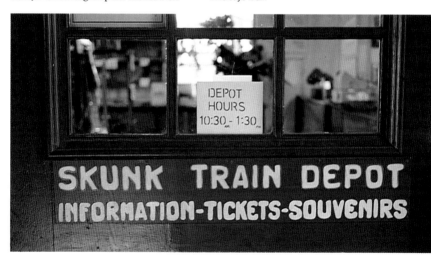

Ghost Towns

The very mention of ghost towns conjures up memories of old Westerns, bleached bones in the desert and tumbleweed blowing through deserted ruins.

California has its fair share of these abandoned settlements. Whenever a mine ran out of gold or silver the town that grew up around it would lose its population. The mines were never in the most hospitable parts of the state and there was absolutely no reason for anyone to live in these God-forsaken places unless there was money to be made.

The buildings usually fell into decay within a few years and often all that can be found now are a few rusty tin cans, barbed wire and the overgrown foundations of a few houses, though occasionally some buildings survived. The most popular and accessible ghost town lies just outside Barstow on the road between Los Angeles and Las Vegas.

In 1881, Calico boomed with 20 saloons and its own Chinatown. Over $86 million of gold and silver was mined before the mines were exhausted.

Walter Knott of Knott's Berry Farm restored the town and handed it over to San Bernardino County who now operate it as a kind of ghost town theme park. In spite of its blatantly commercial atmosphere, you can still get a feel for the harsh life of the miners in these barren mountains.

In 1904, on the edge of Death Valley, a gold strike near Rhyolite resulted in the population growing to 10,000 in a few months. By 1911, the city was reduced to a handful.

Just outside the northwest boundary of Death Valley, Rhyolite today is a group of ruined façades. The front of the Cook Bank Building provides the perfect symbol of a ghost town for photographers, and a few other ruins line the once busy main street. In 1906, Tom Kelly built a house out of 51,000 bottles. Not only is this still standing but it is still inhabited. Inside is an odd collection of antiques and relics.

Bodie is one of the jewels of California. High in the Eastern Sierra at the end of a long stretch of dirt road off Highway 395, Bodie stands as a remarkably well-preserved example of a classic ghost town. Until 1876 it was a thriving mining community. Today

Calico – almost a movie set

The ghost town of Calico

Bodie – classic ghost town

Bodie, in the Eastern Sierra

170 houses still stand and you can wander through streets that have remained unchanged for decades.

This outdoor museum has been designated a State Historic Park and although there has been little renovation, the buildings have been preserved from further deterioration. Many of the buildings are open and many are still complete with furniture and personal belongings. There is a feeling of total authenticity here, particularly when trying to breath the thin mountain air at 8,500 feet as you climb the steep streets.

Opposite the town is a cemetery that graphically documents the lives of the miners.

RUSSIAN RIVER ROAD TOUR

Just over an hour's drive north from San Francisco is the Russian River resort area, which first became popular as a retreat for San Francisco's affluent. Those days are long gone, and the Russian River these days is an eclectic cultural collection. Very popular for tours is **Korbel Champagne Cellars** *(tel: 707 887 2294)* on River Road a few miles east of Guerneville. Noted for its champagnes, this vintage 1886 red brick building (lovely gardens) is the only outlet for the company's table wines. Just north of Guerneville are **Armstrong Redwood State Preserve** and adjacent **Austin Creek State Recreation Area** *(tel: 707 865 2391 for both)*, fine for short strolls.

Some people prefer canoeing: **Burke's Canoe Trips** in Forestville *(tel: 707 887 1222)* offers quite reasonable day-long tours. Others prefer following the river inland to visit abundant and excellent area wineries. Still others consider the Russian River an annual event and visit only in September, during the very popular **Russian River Jazz Festival**. (Big-name talent, bigger crowds.) For information: **Russian River Chamber of Commerce,** *P O Box 331, Guerneville, CA 95441 (tel: 707 869 9009)*. For a free map and brochure about area wineries, contact: **Russian River Wine Road,** *P O Box 127, Guerneville, CA 95441 (tel: 707 433 6935)*.

SAILING ON HORSEBACK

The one-time ranch of noted American adventurer and author Jack London is now open to the public, preserved as an exceptional state historic park. With his wife Charmian, London regularly travelled the grasslands and wooded canyons of his beloved Beauty Ranch on horseback. 'I am a sailor on horseback!' he once declared. Especially enjoyable today, and historically appropriate, are the horseback rides offered here. For information: **Sonoma Cattle Company,** *P O Box 877, Glen Ellen, CA 95442 (tel: 707 996 8566)*.

In the Russian River's Armstrong Redwoods another company offers half-day to three-day horseback trips as noted for the campfire cuisine as for the well-mannered mountain-savvy horses. For information: **Armstrong Woods Pack Station,** *P O Box 970, Guerneville, CA 95446 (tel: 707 887 2939)*.

In Big Sur, rides in Andrew Molera State Park and longer into the Ventana Wilderness are offered by former Esalen psychologist Nevada Robertson, who knows the area almost as well as she understands horses. For information: **Big Sur Trail Rides,** *P O Box 111, Big Sur, CA 93920 (tel: 408 667 2666)*.

SKY HIGH IN GLIDERS

Generally called sailplaning in the US, some people enjoy sailing through the air in an airplane *sans* engine. It is very quiet, and the views are astounding. To experience the thrill of gliding over California's wine country, head toward Calistoga (advance reservations advised). For information: **Calistoga Gliders,** *1546 Lincoln Avenue, Calistoga, CA 94515 (tel: 707 942 5000)*.

SPELUNKING INTO MIDDLE EARTH

California has fascinating caves and caverns to explore, most of them in the Gold Country foothills. All have civilised descent via steps or stairways. A few also allow adventurers to abseil down into the primal darkness.

East of San Andreas, visitors to **California Caverns** *(tel: 209-736 2708)* can spurn the commercial 'trail of lights'' at this state historic landmark and instead squeeze through muddy fissures to reach hidden caves and underground lakes (hardhats, overalls, rafts, and guides provided). To the south, near Murphys, **Mercer Caverns** *(tel: 209 728 2101)* is strictly a family destination. But at **Moaning Cavern** near Angels Camp *(tel: 209 736 2708)* no experience is required for the more exciting abseil route or full caving tour. (This cave is reputedly the largest in California, with the huge main cavern large enough to hide the statue of Liberty.) Hundreds of miles north are the **Lake Shasta Caverns** *(tel :916 238 2341)*. Abseiling or rappelling tours of these colourful, caves are by advance booking only.

Sailing on horseback at Mammoth

SANTA CATALINA ISLAND

A mere 22 miles off the coast near Long Beach, Santa Catalina Island provides within its 56 miles of coastline a pristine wilderness that rises to over 2,000 feet in elevation in the interior.

Visitors take the ferry from Long Beach to Avalon, the only town on the island. Maps and information can be obtained from the **Santa Catalina Island Chamber of Commerce**, *tel: 213 510 1520*. Glass-bottom-boat tours are available from several kiosks along Avalon Pleasure Pier. The **Santa Catalina Island Company** *(tel: 213 510 2000)* has night tours when floodlights are used to attract the marine life.

The **Catalina Safari Bus** service *(tel: 213 510 2800)* drops off hikers at various points around the island.

Bicycles can be rented from **Brown's Bikes** at *107 Pebbly Beach Road, Avalon (tel: 213 510 2493)*.

THE WINE TRAIN

Intensely disliked in Napa Valley but popular with tourists is the Wine Train. All runs head north from the city of Napa to St Helena, where passengers disembark for winery tours by bus. More expensive trips include food served in the dining cars, while hors d'oeuvres and wine tasting are offered in the lounge cars. Closed Mondays. For information: **Napa Valley Wine Train**, *1275 McKinstry Street, Napa, CA 94559 (tel: 707 253 2111 or toll-free in California 800 522 4142)*.

WHALE-WATCHING

From mid-December until the end of February, the California gray whale makes its annual 6,000-mile migration from Alaska to Mexico. They return between March and mid-May.

These huge mammals can be seen from many of the promontories along the coast or, for a more intimate experience, travel out to meet them in a small boat. Whale-watching cruises are run by several companies including: **The Oceanic Society** *(tel: 415 474 3385)*, **King Salmon Charters** *(tel: 707 442 3474)* and **New Sea Angler and Jaws** *(tel: 707 875 3495)*.

Shopping

*C*alifornia is a shopper's dream. Not only can you find anything and everything but the price will be attractive too.

Union Street, San Francisco

Clothes

Both men's and women's clothes are available in a wide variety of styles and prices from French designer dresses and Savile Row suits to denim jeans. There are some incredible bargains to be found if you know where to look.

J C Penny and Montgomery Ward are both department store chains that have very inexpensive clothes. You will not find anything approaching *haute couture* but for work clothes they are difficult to beat.

At the other end of the department store ladder are Macy's, Nordstrom and Sak's Fifth Avenue which have designer clothes and recognised brand names. These stores often have sales offering good savings. Local newspapers will always feature large display ads for these sales.

There are several discount clothing stores that offer the best bargains of all. They all sell name brands, often designer labels, and often factory seconds. They may not have a wide range of sizes available in all styles but their prices more than make up for the lack of choice.

The cheapest is **Ross Dress for Less** for both men's and women's clothes. For men, **The Men's Warehouse** has very good quality suits and jackets as do **C & R Clothiers,** and for women **The Clothes Time** has a good selection. Outlet stores are operated by manufacturers who feature their seconds and discontinued lines at very low prices.

For the height of fashion and designs from the *couture* houses there is no shortage of shops; Beverly Hills' **Rodeo Drive** is full of them, but do not expect low prices. In San Francisco, **Jessica McClintock** and **Obiko** for women's fashion and **Wilkes Bashford** for men represent this top end of the market.

Electronic Goods

Remember that all equipment powered by mains electricity will be for 110v at 60 cycles, but battery-powered gadgets use internationally available battery sizes.

As the home of America's hi-tech industry, California has plenty of computer peripherals and software at bargain prices. Determine compatibility with overseas systems first.

Photographic Equipment

The US is currently one of the cheapest places in the world to buy cameras and lenses, but always check on the lowest prices first. *Popular Photography,* a monthly magazine, carries dozens of ads offering equipment at discount prices. These are usually from New York but they will give an idea of a reasonable price range. Many shops will negotiate rather than lose a sale.

Avoid shops in tourist areas which may try to take advantage of unsuspecting foreigners. **Whole Earth Access** is a New Age department store which will match any locally advertised price for any of the wide range of equipment they carry.

Cameras in the US frequently have a different designation from the rest of the world. The Nikon 8008 is the identical camera to the Nikon 801, for example, but the shop assistant may not know. If you plan to buy an expensive item check on the specifications before you leave home.

Remember too that the US designation will make it obvious to customs officials where an item was purchased, so keep the receipt handy for when you travel abroad again.

Film of all makes, types and formats is widely available at very low prices.

Books and Music

Discounting books has become an accepted practice in the US and many newly published works are available at substantial discounts. **Crown Books** is one of the largest discount chains.

LPs are now virtually unobtainable but there is no shortage of cassettes and compact discs. **Tower Records** and **The Wharehouse** have the greatest selection and the best prices.

Souvenirs

Apart from the obvious printed T-shirt and mugs, there is little that is unique to California. The Disney Store, not only at Disneyland but also in a dozen other locations throughout the state, has excellent Disney memorabilia. Gold nugget jewellery is a popular souvenir of the Gold Country, and 'grow your own redwood' kits make interesting mementoes – if you have room for the world's tallest tree!

For the sports fan, clothing in the colours of both major baseball and American football clubs is available at most sports outfitters.

Museum shops generally have very high-quality merchandise that is well designed, functional and frequently educational.

GREATER LOS ANGELES

Southern California is the home of vast shopping malls. The largest is **Del Amo** in Torrence, and others include the **Glendale Village** and **Santa Monica Mall.** The shops and department stores within these malls are virtually interchangeable.

Beverly Center

This is an eight-acre shopping mall filled with up-market shops, department stores and restaurants.

Farmer's Market

Although farmers are unlikely to make the journey here these days there are still impressive food displays at over 160 outlets throughout this open-air complex.

Fisherman's Village

This re-creation of a New England fishing village has the usual collection of gift and souvenir shops.

Melrose Avenue
The 6000 and 7000 blocks of Melrose Avenue have some of the craziest off-the-wall shops in California. It is, however, extremely chic.

Olvera Street
In the heart of old Lost Angeles is a vibrant, brick-paved street lined with shops and street vendors selling Mexican food and arts and crafts from Mexico.

Ports O'Call Village
This mock 19th-century fishing village has dozens of shops overlooking Los Angeles Harbor at San Pedro.

Rodeo Drive
The name is synonymous with wealth. Window-shopping along this super-exclusive street is enough for most people. Some of the shops even have locked doors and only admit customers by appointment. Nearly every major designer has a shop along Rodeo Drove including Cartier, Gucci and Armani.

Westwood Village
Located next to the UCLA campus, this is the premier shopping area in west Los Angeles. It caters to both college students and fashionable Westside residents. The bookstores are particularly good.

SAN DIEGO

Bazaar del Mundo
This Mexican market-place is within Old Town San Diego State Park. A wide range of the colourful arts and crafts of Mexico are on sale.

Horton Plaza
Not only is this an architectural

The Crocker Galleria

masterpiece, it is one of the best examples of a user-friendly shopping mall in the US. Over 140 shops and restaurants provide for every shopper's need.

Gaslamp Quarter
The old buildings of this historic district are now home to several antique shops and art galleries.

Seaport Village
Over 65 shops occupy this new waterfront development close to downtown San Diego.

SAN FRANCISCO

The Cannery
This converted Del Monte canning factory, close to Fisherman's Wharf, has three floors of boutiques and restaurants centred around a landscaped courtyard.

Crocker Galleria
The Galleria in Milan was the model for this glass-domed collection of 60 fashionable shops selling designer fashions and elegant gifts.

Ghirardelli Square
Ghirardelli still keep a small part of their famous chocolate factory operating, but most of it has been transformed into a multi-level shopping complex with an interesting mixture of boutiques, galleries and restaurants.

Grant Avenue
For eight blocks there are dozens of Chinese craft shops, jewellers and Asian bazaars. Many of the goods are cheap imports but occasionally you can strike lucky and find a treasure. Remember the Chinese saying that the best goods are never at the front.

Maiden Lane
Several exclusive boutiques and art galleries line this charming lane off Union Square. The most notable building, No 140, was designed by Frank Lloyd Wright.

Pier 39
The best street performers in the city entertain the shoppers on this old San Francisco cargo wharf that now has two levels of shops.

San Francisco Center
One of San Francisco's newest shopping experiences is this nine-storey vertical mall crowned by a five-storey branch of Nordstrom's.

Sutter Street
For four blocks, from the 300s to the 700s, Sutter Street has some of the most exclusive fashion boutiques and art galleries in northern California.

Union Street
Not to be confused with Union Square, this street in the Cow Hollow neighbourhood is full of small, fashionable boutiques and curio shops.

Union Square
If San Francisco has a centre, then this is it. All the major department stores are here including exclusive Neiman-Marcus. Just off the square on Post Street, Gumps has a range of furnishings, oriental antiques and homeware.

OTHER AREAS
Surprisingly, one of the finest shopping streets in the US, equalling Rodeo Drive in quality, is **El Paseo** in Palm Desert. Art galleries, high-fashion boutiques, jewellers, exclusive antique dealers and fine restaurants all rub shoulders along this extravagant street.

In nearby Palm Springs, the **Desert Fashion Plaza** houses high-class department stores, boutiques and jewellers.

Relaxation at Ghirardelli Square

Entertainment

*I*n the state that is the centre of the world's film industry, there is no shortage of talent waiting to make its mark on the world of entertainment. It seems that every restaurant in Los Angeles is staffed by actors and actresses just waiting to be discovered.

Both London West End and Broadway shows are regularly featured at theatres in Los Angeles and San Francisco, and these are complemented by a multitude of small theatres producing both experimental and traditional drama. Comedy clubs are particularly good.

Music inevitably has a strong representation; many rock stars have made their home in Los Angeles or the San Francisco area. Mill Valley alone, a town of less than 15,000 people, is home to The Grateful Dead, Jefferson Starship, Huey Lewis, Maria Muldur, Sammy Hagar and other great musicians. **The Sweetwater Saloon** on Throckmorton Avenue in Mill Valley features live music every night, and many of these local musicians often drop in to jam with the featured band.

Classical fans are well catered for with world-class opera, ballet and symphony orchestras.

Newspapers almost always have entertainment pages both listing and reviewing current happenings. San Francisco is particularly well served. The Pink Section of the Sunday edition of the *San Francisco Chronicle* has a detailed listing of virtually every event for the week for northern California.

Also in San Francisco, **KFOG, a radio station have an Entertainment Line** at *415 543 1045* and the **BASS** ticket agency has a recorded events calendar at *510 762 2277*.

Day-of-performance tickets are available at half price from the **San Francisco Ticket Box Office** in Union Square, on Stockton Street between Post and Geary *(tel: 415 433 7827)*.

In Los Angeles, the *Los Angeles Times* has a daily calendar section that gives complete listings of events and performances in the Greater Los Angeles area. The Sunday edition has an expanded calendar section.

Throughout the year there are events taking place from county fairs and rodeos to film and jazz festivals. The dates and venues are different every year but the **California Office of Tourism** can provide detailed current listings of all the major events.

MAJOR THEATRES

Los Angeles
Ahmanson Theater, *135 North Grand Avenue (tel: 213 410 1062)*
Coronet Theater, *366 North La Cienega Boulevard (tel: 213 659 2400)*
Wilshire Ebell Theater, *4401 West 8th Street (tel: 213 939 1128)*

San Diego
La Jolla Playhouse, *UCSD Campus (tel: 619 534 3960)*
Old Globe Theater, *Balboa Park (tel: 619 236 2255)*
San Diego Repertory Theater, *79 Horton Plaza (tel: 619 235 8025)*

San Francisco
American Conservatory Theater, *450 Geary Street (tel: 415 673 6440)*
Curran Theater, *445 Geary Street (tel: 415 474 3800)*
Golden Gate Theater, *25 Taylor Street (tel: 415 474 3800)*
Orpheum Theater, *1192 Market Street (tel: 435 474 3800)*

San Carlos
Circle Star Theater *1717 Industrial Road (tel: 415 366 7100)*

EXPERIMENTAL AND FRINGE THEATRE

Los Angeles
Celebration Theater, *426 North Hoover Street (tel: 213 876 4257)*
Colony Studio Theater Playhouse, *1944 Riverside Drive (tel: 213 665 3011)*
Los Angeles Theater Center, *514 Spring Street (tel: 213 451 0621)*

San Francisco
Cable Car Theater, *430 Mason Street (tel: 415 421 6162)*

COMEDY CLUBS

Los Angeles
The Comedy Store, *8433 West Sunset Boulevard (tel: 213 656 6225)*
(Also in La Jolla and Westwood)
The Improv, *1862 Melrose Avenue (tel: 213 651 2583)*

Encino
LA Caberet Comedy Club, *17271 Ventura Boulevard (tel: 818 501 3737)*

San Francisco
Cobb's, *2069 Chestnut Street (tel: 415 928 4320)*

Josie's Cabaret and Juice Joint, *3583 16th Street (tel: 415 861 7933)*
The Punch Line, *444 Battery Street (tel: 415 379 7573)*

MAGIC
Merlin McFly's, *2702 Main Street, Santa Monica (tel: 213 392 8468)*

CLASSICAL MUSIC, BALLET AND OPERA

Los Angeles
The Beverly Theater, *9404 Wilshire Boulevard (tel: 213 410 1062)*
The Music Center, *135 North Grand Avenue (tel: 213 972 7211)*
Wiltern Theater, *3790 Wilshire Boulevard (tel: 213 380 5005)*

San Diego
San Diego Opera, *202 C Street (tel: 619 232 7636)*
San Diego Symphony, *1245 7th Avenue (tel: 619 699 4200)*

San Francisco
San Francisco Opera and Ballet, *War Memorial Opera House, Van Ness Avenue (tel: 415 864 3330)*
San Francisco Symphony, *Davies Hall, Van Ness Avenue (tel: 415 621 3838)*

JAZZ
The Baked Potato, *3787 Cahuenga Boulevard, N. Hollywood (tel: 818 980 1615)*
The Central, *88852 Sunset Boulevard, Hollywood (tel: 213 652 5937)*
Linda's, *6715 Melrose Avenue (tel: 213 934 6199)*
Kimball's East, *5800 Shellmound Street, Emeryville (tel: 510 658 2555)*

EVENTS

January
Rosebowl Parade, Pasedena

February
Chinese New Year, San Francisco and Los Angeles

March
Santa Barbara International Film Festival
Santa Cruz Jazz Festival

April
Redding Dixieland Jazz Festival
Cherry Blossom Festival, San Francisco

May
Cinco de Mayo throughout the state
La Fiesta de San Luis Obispo
Rodeo week, Redding

June
Old Globe Shakespearian Festival, San Diego
Flower Festival, Lompoc

July
California Rodeo, Salinas
Carmel Bach Festival
Steinbeck Festival, Salinas
Sonoma County Fair
International Surf Festival – southern California beaches

August
Mozart Festival, San Luis Obispo
Monterey County Fair

September
California State Fair
Sausalito Arts Festival
Monterey Jazz Festival

October
Fleet Week, San Francisco
Grand National Rodeo, San Francisco

November
Death Valley Days

December
Christmas at the Adobes, Monterey

CABARET

Los Angeles
Chippendale's, *3739 Overland Avenue, W. Los Angeles (tel: 213 396 4045)*
Cinefrill, *7000 Hollywood Boulevard, Hollywood (tel: 213 466 7000)*
La Cage aux Folles, *634 North La Cienega Boulevard, Hollywood (tel: 213 657 1091)*
Romeo and Juliet, *435 North Beverly Drive, Beverly Hills (tel: 213 273 2292)*
Great American Music Hall, *859 O'Farrell Street (tel: 415 885 0750)*

DANCING AND ROCK

Los Angeles
Club Lingerie, *6507 Sunset Boulevard, Hollywood (tel: 213 466 8557)*

Gazzarris, *9039 Sunset Boulevard, Hollywood (tel: 213 273 2222)*
The Palace, *1735 North Vine Street, Hollywood (tel: 213 472 3000)*

San Diego
Fat City, *2137 Pacific Highway (tel: 619 232 0686)*
Belly Up, *143 S. Cedros Avenue, Solana Beach (tel: 619 481 9022)*

San Francisco
Club DV8, *55 Natoma Street (tel: 415 957 1730)*
The I-Beam, *1748 Haight Street (tel: 415 668 6006)*
The Oasis, *11th and Folsom Street (tel: 415 621 8119)*
Slim's, *333 11th Street, San Francisco (tel: 415 621 3330)*

ENTERTAINMENT FOR CHILDREN

California is a children's paradise. From Disneyland on there is a multitude of activities to keep even the most jaded children amused for days. It would be impossible to cover everything here as almost every entry in the book would be suitable. Below are listed just a few of the attractions not mentioned elsewhere.

Apart from Disneyland (see Los Angeles) there are several theme parks that provide endless thrills for kids with strong stomachs.

Knott's Berry Farm

This is the father of all theme parks and it is next door to Disneyland in Buena Park (see Buena Park).
Tel: 714 827 1776
Open: daily, 10am–6pm in winter;
10am–midnight in summer.

Marine World Africa USA

One of the major attractions here is the ease with which the children can interact with the animals. Several shows are given throughout the day including a killer whale, tigers, dolphins and California sea lions. Children under 12 can crawl through the inside of a life-size replica of a blue whale.
Marine World Parkway, Vallejo (tel: 707
643 6722). Open: summer, daily,
9.30am–6pm; September to May,
Wednesday to Sunday, 9.30am–5pm.

Marriott's Great America

This park in Santa Clara County south of San Francisco offers a similar assortment of rides to most theme parks and, although the names are changed, the thrills remain the same.
Great America Parkway, Santa Clara (tel:
408 988 1800). Open: daily, from
Memorial Day to Labor Day; weekends
during spring and autumn; closed winter.

Six Flags Magic Mountain

The ultimate amusement park where, for one-price admission, children (and adults) can get their fill of some of the most hair-raising thrill rides in California.

Over 100 different rides spread across 260 acres and include the Colossus, one of the biggest and, at 60 mph, fastest wooden roller-coasters in the world. Other roller-coasters in the park include Viper, Revolution and Ninja! There are gentler rides for young children, and a dolphin and sea lion show.
26101 Magic Mountain Parkway, Valencia
(tel: 805 255 4111).
Open: winter, weekends, 10am–6pm;
summer, daily from 10am.

Winchester Mystery House

Children love the bizarre and spooky atmosphere of the house. It was built by Sarah Winchester, heiress to the Winchester rifle fortune. She believed that she would live as long as the house continued to grow. When she died in 1922 there were 160 rooms covering 6 acres. Doors open on to blank walls, stairways lead nowhere, and ghost stories abound.
325 Winchester Boulevard, San Jose (tel:
408 247 2101).
Open: hours vary with the season.

The **Pickle Family Circus** performs at different venues in San Francisco throughout the year *(telephone 415 826 0747).*

Children's theatre and special events are always regularly held in many parts of the state, and newspapers give listings with full detail.

Sport

California is the home of champions, a breeding ground for athletes of every kind and state with an unparalleled sports infrastructure churning out some of the world's best athletes.

With its nearly ideal weather condtions and its penchant for the pursuit of perfection when it comes to all things physical, California is an athlete's Mecca. It has 14 major professional sports teams, dozens of minor league teams, some of the best collegiate athletics in the country and a huge variety of opportunity for participant sports. Nearly one-third of American athletes at the 1988 Summer Olympics were native Californians. They won 30 medals–32 per cent of the US total. Observes author Herbert Gold, 'This Dorado of escapees from elsewhere has produced a new race – the Californian. So much athletic grace is almost unnatural.'

To be a good sport in California, you can either do it or just watch it. Whatever you choose, it is all around to you.

SPECTATOR SPORTS

AMERICAN FOOTBALL
No other state can boast having as many professional football teams as California. Four teams from the National Football League take to the field (called the gridiron) every autumn from early September through to late December. Two lucky teams go all the way to the Super Bowl in January

The **San Francisco 49ers**, with one of the best records in recent football history, play at Candlestick Park *(tel: 415 468 2249)*. Since 1981, the 49ers have won four Super Bowl titles behind the leadership on one of the sport's greatest players ever, Joe Montana.

College football – just as exciting

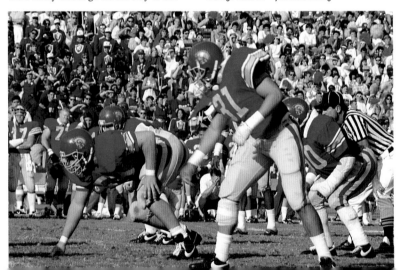

Because of their great success, getting a ticket to a 49ers game is difficult. They are nearly always sold out.

The **Los Angeles Rams**, who play their home games at the Anaheim Stadium *(tel: 213 937 6767)* have hit hard times in recent years, though the team has a great and colourful history.

Also in Los Angeles are the **Raiders**, one of the most feared teams in the National Football League because of their aggressive and hard-hitting style of football. They play at the Los Angeles Memorial Coliseum, where the 1932 and 1984 Olympic Games were held *(tel: 213 322 5901)*.

The **San Diego Chargers** battle on the field at Jack Murphy Stadium *(tel: 619 280 2111)*.

College football is also quite enjoyable and accessible. In northern California, both Stanford University *(tel: 415 497 1021)* and the University of California at Berkeley *(tel: 510 642 5150)* have strong football traditions. In southern **California, the University of Southern California, University of California** at Los Angeles and **San Diego State University** are among a host of college teams to take the field. Southern California also boasts one of football's great traditions, the **Rose Bowl,** which is held each 1 January between the best teams in the two major athletic divisions. Each year 3,500 seats are sold in a random draw. Send a postcard to: **Rose Bowl Ticket Drawing,** *PO Box 7122, Pasadena, CA 91109,* postmarked between 15 September and 15 October. For information, call *213 793 7193.*

BASEBALL

The American equivalent to cricket takes place at five major baseball league stadiums across California. From April to October, the teams, from both the American League and National League, bat it out on Astroturf and natural grass, playing about 80 home games each.

In the San Francisco Bay area, two of the nation's best teams, the **San Francisco Giants** and the **Oakland Athletics,** play a brand of baseball known as Bays ball. The Giants swing their bats at Candlestick Park *(tel: 415 467 8000)*. The Athletics, winners of the 1989 World Series – the famous series that was interrupted by the 7.1 Loma

College baseball at USC

Prieta earthquake – play in the Oakland Coliseum *(tel: 510 638 0500)*.

In southern California, a strong baseball tradition has grown and transformed at least a portion of the laid-back, beach-going populace into rabid, hot-dog-eating fans of the baseball field.

The **Los Angeles Dodgers** enjoy an outstanding reputation in baseball and often lead the league in attendance. They play at Dodger Stadium *(tel: 213 224 1400)*.

The **California Angels** play at the Anaheim Stadium *(tel: 714 634 2000)* and the **San Diego Padres** play at Jack Murphy Stadium *(tel: 619 283 4494)*.

BASKETBALL

The regular National Basketball Association season runs from October until April, with championship playoffs continuing until May.

The **Golden State Warriors** play at the Oakland Coliseum Arena *(tel: 415 638 6000)*, where they play an average of 40 home games each season. In the state capital, the **Sacramento Kings** are an up-and-coming team, full of enthusiasm, but as of yet they have not been able to muster much in the way of wins.

The **Los Angeles Clippers** are also struggling towards success, but as a young team they have shown promise in recent years.

The reigning champions of California basketball remain the **Los Angeles Lakers,** who play at the Forum in Inglewood *(tel: 213 673 1300)*. One of the greatest teams in the history of American sport, the Lakers have developed a following that literally spans the globe. Jerry West and Kareem Abdul Jabar are among the team's greatest players. But the most famous Laker of all is without question Earvin 'Magic' Johnson, the man who invented such moves as the no-loss pass, the triple double and the coast to coast, but whose career was tragically affected when he was diagnosed in 1991 as being HIV positive.

ICE HOCKEY

In a state where surf and sunshine dominate the landscape, ice hockey, known simply as hockey in the US, seems somewhat out of place. From October to April, the National Hockey League invades California. The **Los**

A perfect start

Angeles Kings, strong championship contenders, play at the Forum in Inglewood. Wayne Gretzky, considered by many to be the greatest player the game has ever seen, joined the Kings in 1989 and has led the team to its greatest record ever.

The **San Jose Sharks** joined the National Hockey League as recently as 1991 and have consistently provided the Bay Area fans with bloodthirsty action with its own brand of Shark Hockey. The Sharks play at the new San Jose arena.

HORSE RACING

Lady Luck and good old-fashioned love of horses bring thousands of spectators out to California's racetracks, where you can wager as little as $2 on your favourite contender.

In northern California, **Bay Meadows** in San Mateo is one of the state's classic ovals. Thoroughbred horses race from mid-September to early February, while quarter horses run from February to early May. **Golden Gate Fields** holds thoroughbred races from February to late June.

The Sears Point racetrack near Napa

Three tracks dominate activities in southern California. **Hollywood Park** hosts thoroughbred races from April to July and harness racing from August to December.

Santa Ana Park holds thoroughbred races from December to April, while the season at the **Del Mar Track** in San Diego runs from mid-July to early September.

MOTOR RACING

Every April, the US Grand Prix for 500cc motorcycles takes place at **Laguna Seca** near Monterey. Long Beach holds a grand prix for Indy cars every year and in San Diego, at the Del Mar racetrack, there are IMSA car races which are the equivalent to European Class C cars.

Sears Point International Raceway near Napa holds race meets for both cars and motorcycles from February to September. The popular NASCAR championship takes place here and also the SCCA TransAm Race. A racing school operates throughout the year for budding racing drivers.

Scenic Mammoth golf course

PARTICIPANT SPORTS

GOLF

If you decide to bring your clubs on holiday, you will not be disappointed. Golf is a year-round sport in nearly all parts of California, and almost every city and town has a public golf course. In southern California alone there are more than 200 public courses.

Several courses stand out and deserve special mention.

Pebble Beach near Carmel is a world-class resort with world-class views and world-class prices. Green fees are $200 per player! Everything else at this semi-private resort, owned by Japanese interests but on state-owned land, is also expensive. Yet the scenery and the challenging course are magnificent and

definitely a once-in-a-lifetime experience for the avid golfer.

A tremendous assortment of other public courses dot the California landscape and include: **Silverado Country Club** in Napa, **Tilden Park** in Berkeley, **Cypress Point** in Monterey, **Sean Ranch** near Mendocino, **Rancho Park Golf Course** (the site of the Los Angeles Open), **Torrey Pines Municipal Golf Course** in La Jolla and the **Palm Springs Municipal Golf Course**.

The Yellow Pages has listings of both public and private golf courses.

TENNIS

California is tennis crazy. At nearly every school and every park in California, players both old and young practise their skills in what might be the nation's leading tennis state. From Pancho Gonzales and Jack Kramer to Tracy Austin and Billie Jean King, California has dominated the sport of tennis, on both professional and amateur levels.

The Yellow Pages lists private clubs and occasionally public courts. Many towns have municipal courts and these can be found by telephoning the appropriate parks and recreation departments listed under the Government Pages in the telephone directory.

More information on tennis can be obtained from the Northern California Tennis Association *(tel: 510 748 7373)* or the Southern California Tennis Association *(tel: 310 208 3838)*.

SKIING

Whether you are a downhill skier or a cross-country skier, California has some of the finest conditions in the US. From November to May, skiing in the Sierra

Nevada has gathered a national following. It is almost always better than the cold, icy and crowded ski slopes of the East Coast; it is often every bit as good as the famed Rocky Mountain skiing.

The Lake Tahoe region, with 20 ski areas and 160 lifts, boasts the highest concentration of skiing in the US. Resorts include **Squaw Valley, Heavenly Valley, Kirkwood** and **Alpine Meadows**.

Further south is **Mammoth Mountain,** on the eastern side of the Sierras. It is one of the continent's largest ski areas, with 30 lifts and more than 150 trails, with a vertical drop of 3,300 feet. Nearer Los Angeles, an assortment of ski areas include **Mount Baldy, Big Bear, Snow Summit, Mount Waterman** and **Krata Ridge**.

Cross-country skiing is also very popular in the Sierras. You can ski at a touring centre such as the **Kirkwood Touring Center** near Lake Tahoe. For the more intrepid, a trip into the backcountry in one of the state's many mountain parks and reserves is a possibility.

OTHER SPORTS

Watersports are very popular during the summer, including **kayaking** and **white-water rafting. Surfing,** together with **wind surfing,** still enjoy tremendous popularity and **scuba-diving** trips are available at many places along the coast. In the wine country **ballooning** is a popular pastime and several companies offer champagne flights in the early morning. **Hang-gliding** courses are available along the coast for the more adventurous.

Bicycling has gained in popularity since the development of the all-terrain mountain bike. Many National Forests and state parks have designated bike trails.

Horses can be rented at stables located throughout the state, particularly in the coastal areas where the horses can be ridden along the beach.

Fishing, last but certainly not least, is the state's most popular pastime and almost every stretch of water, both fresh and sea, will have an angling club close by. Equipment is usually available for hire by the day at very reasonable rates.

Wherever there is a harbour along the coast someone will be offering fishing charters. Listings of operators can be

Heavenly Valley at Lake Tahoe

found in the Yellow Pages under Fishing Parties. Salmon is the most popular catch, followed by rock cod and bass.

Freshwater fishermen have the choice of steelhead, salmon, sturgeon and trout. Most of the mountain areas have outfitters offering fishing trips and these can again be found in the *Yellow Pages*.

For current information on fishing licences and seasons, contact the **Department of Fish and Game,** *3211 S Street, Sacramento, California 95816 (tel: 916 739 3380).*

See also **Getting Away From it All pages.**

Food and Drink

*W*ithout any exaggeration, there is virtually no cuisine on earth that cannot be found in California. San Francisco alone has over 4,000 restaurants, even more per capita than New York.

Californians enjoy eating, not just for the sake of it but for the love of it. It is a state of 'foodies' who have helped California become one of the world's great gastronomic centres.

Fattening fancies at Chez Panisse

Fine restaurants abound, and not just in the cities. Oakhurst lies between Fresno and the High Sierra, in the middle of nowhere, but even here there is a restaurant that the eminent American gastronome Craig Clairborne deems worthy of visiting – from New York! **Erna's Elderberry House** ($$$$) *(tel: 209 683 6800)* is the unlikely name for this outstanding European restaurant which serves a nightly fixed menu with a choice of either vegetarian or non-vegetarian fare.

It is ridiculous, however, to suggest that all California restaurants are good. There are vast numbers of eating establishments that rely more on quantity than quality and serve unimaginative, greasy American food at its worst.

Some American eating habits are curious, to say the least. Biscuits are like scones and they are usually served smothered in thick white gravy – very often for breakfast! The use of fruit is interesting too. Fruit is considered an appropriate accompaniment to any meal, so do not be too surprised when your bacon and eggs are served with a fruit salad on the same plate.

Some restaurant language can be confusing, so here is a short course on menu translation.

Au jus: usually applied to beef sandwiches served with a dip of beef juices

BLT: toasted bacon, lettuce and tomato sandwich

Broiled: grilled

Brownie: individual chocolate cake

Buffalo wings: chicken wings in a hot and spicy sauce

Chips: potato crisps

Cider: a non-alcoholic apple drink

Club Sandwich: a double-decker sandwich

Eggs Benedict: popular brunch dish of poached eggs on a bed of spinach with an English muffin and covered in Hollandaise sauce

English Muffin: a bit like a crumpet, served toasted

Entré: main course

Fries: chips

Half-and-half: half milk, half cream

Hash browns: fried grated potato

Home or steak fries: thick chips often made with unpeeled potatoes

Jello: jelly

Jelly: jam

Mayo: mayonnaise

Muffin: an individual cake, often made with bran and blueberries

Pancakes: thick batter cakes, served for breakfast with butter and syrup

Prime rib: standing rib of beef served in thick slices

Coffee-shop indulgence

Pudding: a soft, whipped dessert, often of chocolate

Sherbet: sorbet with a milk base

Soda: any soft drink

Sub: submarine – long sandwich made with French bread

Sweet and Low: non-sugar sweetener for coffee, etc.

The restaurant business has always been precarious and has become increasingly so in the present economic climate. New restaurants open and close with monotonous regularity. Apart from the inexpensive chains, all of the restaurants mentioned are well established but tend to be more expensive than most. Always ask locally for recommendations of current popular restaurants.

The following table is an indication of restaurant price. The $ sign represents the cost of a 3-course meal without wine.

$ under $15

$$ under $25

$$$ under $50

$$$$ over $50

Compared with Europe even the most expensive restaurants will seem reasonably priced.

Bread advertisement

FAST FOOD

Fast-food chains abound and many of them are so international that they have become synonymous with American food. **MacDonalds, Kentucky Fried Chicken** and **Pizza Hut** (all $) dominate the world market and they are equally dominant in California. They will provide very cheap, fast food in hygienic surroundings. Fortunately, American tastes and attitudes have been changing in the past decade and the greasy hamburgers with French fries (chips are potato crisps) are now having to compete with chicken breast sandwiches and salads. Even the traditional beef fat for frying French fries has been replaced with vegetable oil in most places and MacDonalds have introduced a low-fat hamburger, the Maclean Burger.

There are several MacDonald look-likes, including **Wendy's, Burger King** and **Jack in the Box** (all $). They all provide variations of the same products at more or less the same price.

COFFEE SHOPS

The coffee shop chains are one step above the fast-food operations and include **Denny's, Bobs Big Boy** and Baker's Square (all $$). While they all serve perfectly edible food it will never be memorable. They are often open 24 hours a day and absolutely predictable. To experience one Denny's is to know them all. They all have inexpensive children's menus and you need never feel embarrassed at having screaming children at your table.

One of the better chains, not really in the coffee shop category except in price, is **The Sizzler** ($$). One of the best eating bargains in California is their all-you-can-eat fruit and salad bar where,

for a ridiculously low price, you can fill yourself on fresh fruit and every kind of fresh salad imaginable. They also cater for children and serve good, inexpensive steaks, chicken and fish. Sizzler restaurants are only open for lunch and dinner.

DINERS

The diner is a very American institution and even lent its name to a film. Although they are less common in California than the East Coast there are a few about in most towns. They are not a lot different from coffee shops. They are generally smaller, with a long counter to sit at. The traditional diner was designed to look like a railroad dining car with lots of chrome and always a juke box. They always served good, basic, cheap food wthout any frills. There are still a few of these around but beware, California, trendy as ever, has taken the diner to new heights. **The Fog City Diner** (*$$$, tel: 415 982 2000*) in San Francisco, for example, is a yuppiefied version of the original, serving dishes such as grilled pasilla pepper with avocado salsa, and crabcakes with a sherry-cayenne mayonnaise. Great food, but hardly your average diner!

BREAKFAST

Diners and coffee shops (not the chains) are the best places for breakfast, and it is often served 24 hours a day. Eggs are the mainstay and, apart from omelettes, scrambled, boiled and poached eggs, they can be fried either:
Sunny-side up – cooked on one side only
Over easy – flipped over so that the white is fully cooked but the yolk is still runny

Over medium – one step beyond the above
Over hard – both the white and yolk are solid.

The eggs are invariably served with hash-brown potatoes, a choice of sausage, ham or bacon, and a choice of white or wheat bread or an English muffin.

At weekends breakfast is eclipsed by brunch at the better restaurants. Usually served between 10am and 3pm, this leisurely meal is just a glorified breakfast accompanied by champagne.

Coffee is the main breakfast-time brew and it varies dramatically in quality from brown water to something a spoon will stand up in. The cheaper the restaurant the weaker the coffee is a good rule of thumb. This may have something to do with the American tradition of serving unlimited coffee for a single price. The pot is bottomless and your cup will be refilled for as long as you sit. Tea is less popular and it is easy to see why. A cup of tea consists of a tea bag in tepid water. Water will continue to be provided until no more colour can be drained from the bag.

Every part of the meal involves decisions. There is nothing as simple as a cup of tea. Do you want Darjeeling, English breakfast, Earl Grey, Camomile, Constant Comment, Ginseng? The list goes on and on and on. You want milk in it. How about half-and-half, 1 per cent, non-fat, regular vitamin D, non-dairy creamer?

One reason for all this choice is the abundance of produce available in California. As the bread-basket of the nation there is more variety of fresh fruit and vegetables here than in any other state.

In the southern part of the state is a huge citrus industry. The central valley grows everything from avocados to kiwi fruit. Every year there are festivals attracting thousands of people to sample such unlikely dishes as garlic ice cream at the **Gilroy Garlic Festival**. Monterey has a Squid Festival, Castroville hosts an **Artichoke Festival** and Ventura has a slightly more appealing annual **Strawberry Festival**.

Fresh produce is always close at hand and the Pacific provides fish of all shapes and colours. Dungeness crab comes into San Francisco Bay along with swordfish, shark, red snapper, tuna, salmon, squid and many others.

Rockin Robins on Haight Street

BEVERAGES

Wine

The other major crop in California is grapes. The wine industry extends from the great vineyards of Napa and Sonoma up to Lake and Mendocino Counties in the north and as far south as San Diego. Excellent wines are made near Santa Cruz and Santa Barbara that are the equal of many European fine wines. Many of the grapevines, in fact descend from European stock. For example, in Napa Valley the original grapevine cuttings were supplied by priests from the missions at Sonoma and San Rafael.

Most of the California wines are made from a single variety of grape, unlike European wines which are often blends. The wine is named according to the variety, and two that the Californian wine-makers excel at are Cabernet Sauvignon and Chardonnay, but there

A uniquely North American wine

are several other varieties that are eminently drinkable.

No wine-lover should leave California without tasting a good Zinfandel, a grape variety unique to North America. Some of the best Zinfandels are made by Ravenswood and Ridge wineries. A popular trend has been for wineries to follow fashion and produce a white Zinfandel. This rosé wine is pretty to look at but bears little relationship to the big, spicy and fruity red Zinfandels, even though the grape is the same.

Wines are available in any supermarket, any drugstore and, of course, specialised wine merchants. The enormous displays can be confusing to the uninitiated. In restaurants ask for advice, and do not be embarrassed to send the wine back if you think the advice was bad. In shops, on the display, there is often a description and rating of the wine by either a magazine called *The Wine Spectator* or Robert Parker, a well-known American wine writer. The ratings are somewhat controversial because of their subjectivity, but they provide a pretty reliable guide to quality. Generally, any wine that scores over 90 is going to be good.

In cheaper restaurants, particularly outside the main urban areas, the choice will be red, white or burgundy. All will be served straight from the refrigerator. The red will be white Zinfandel or an equally insipid rosé. It is unlikely that any of them will be drinkable.

Beer

America's contribution to the wine industry unfortunately did not spill over to beer. To Europeans, American beer is fizzy and tasteless. Fortunately, in

California there are alternatives. Almost every restaurant and bar will have imported beers available. Heineken and Carlsberg are the most common but the Mexican beers are more interesting and include Dos Equis, Corona, Bohemia and Tecate.

Northern California produces two of the best beers in the US from small local breweries. Sierra Nevada Ale from Chico and San Francisco's Anchor Steam Beer are both excellent. There has been a recent trend in micro-breweries with beer made on the premises. If you can find one of these it is worth a try.

Other Drinks
In non-alcoholic drinks colas lead the market. Both Coke and Pepsi are universally available along with 7-Up, Sprite and Dr Peppers, and they are all available in a sugar-free version. Root beer has a loyal following and connoisseurs rank A&W as one of the best, but it is something of an acquired taste. For the more sophisticated palate, California has several different mineral waters that are either plain or flavoured with different fresh-fruit juices. The most common are Calistoga and Crystal Geyser. They are all refreshing, tasty and healthy.

BARS
Most restaurants serve wine and beer, but only a few of the more expensive ones have a full liquor licence, allowing them to sell hard spirits. Serious drinkers have to go to bars, and the American bar is certainly a place for serious drinking. They are almost always dark and have a decidedly decadent air to them. They always seem the kind of place you would not want your mother to see you enter.

Bars generally open as early as 6am

and stay open until 2am. Many bars will advertise a 'Happy Hour' between 5pm and 7pm when drinks are often two for the price of one, and in the better bars free hors-d'oeuvres are served. The food is sometimes so good that it can be a good substitute for dinner.

Be careful – it's potent stuff. This Mexican spirit is made of the distilled fermented juice of an agave plant

CALIFORNIA CUISINE

The revolution in cooking in California started with a small group of northern California chefs who developed dishes using the freshest possible local ingredients and presenting them with a simple elegance. Many Americans used to plates groaning with food criticise the small portions often associated with this American *nouvelle cuisine*.

One of the innovators was Alice Waters whose restaurant in Berkeley, **Chez Panisse** ($$$$), is still a gastronomic Mecca. The restaurant serves a fixed menu nightly and reservations must be made weeks in advance. To experience the cooking without the expense, go upstairs to the **Cafe at Chez Panisse** ($$$). This is an à la carte restaurant that does not take reservations. The wait can be long but the food is worth it.

1517 Shattuck Avenue, Berkeley (tel: 415 548 5525)

Stars ($$$) remains popular, and the **Stars Cafe** ($$$), next door, serves

The plush interior of a San Francisco restaurant

excellent food at realistic prices. Their fish and chips are remarkable.

150 Redwood Street, San Francisco (tel: 415 861 7827)

PosTrio ($$$$) is Wolfgang Puck's San Francisco outpost, and this elegant restaurant serves consistently good food.

545 Post Street, San Francisco (tel: 415 776 7825)

Puck's most famous restaurant is **Spago** ($$$$) in West Hollywood. Along with Chez Panisse this represents the pinnacle of California cuisine.

1114 Horn Avenue, Los Angeles (tel: 213 652 4025)

Other outstanding restaurants:
Citrus $$$$
6703 Melrose Avenue, Los Angeles (tel: 213 939 5354)
Michael's $$$$
1147 Third Street, Santa Monica (tel: 213 451 0843)

EAST–WEST CUISINE

A recent trend has been to combine elements of both fine Oriental and Western cooking. A few restaurants have done with this great success.

Chinois East-West $$$
2232 Fair Oaks Boulevard, Sacramento (tel: 415 775 4789)
China Moon Cafe $$$
639 Post Street, San Francisco (tel: 415 775 4789)
Chinois on Main $$$$
2709 Main Street, Santa Monica (tel: 213 392 9025)

The Massawa on Haight Street

RESTAURANTS OF THE WORLD

The ubiquitous Chinese restaurant excels in California, particularly in San Francisco where a huge Chinese community supports some of the best in

The Fior d'Italia, Washington Square

the world. Drop into almost any of the tiny restaurants scattered throughout Chinatown and the Avenues for delicious Chinese food from virtually every kind of produce.

Japanese restaurants abound in both the LA and San Francisco Japantowns. They are completely authentic and serve everything from noodle dishes to fresh sushi. **The Benihana of Tokyo** chain ($$$) cook food at the table, and what the food lacks in imagination is more than compensated by the entertainment.

Italian restaurants are extremely popular throughout California and range from very inexpensive to ultra de-luxe, but there us a broad middle range serving excellent food.

French restaurants are more difficult to find and they are generally in the higher price bracket. The best are as good as you can find anywhere. Masa's ($$$$) in San Francisco has consistently been rated as one of the top 10 best restaurants in the US.

For value, the South-East Asian restaurants cannot be beaten. Vietnamese and Thai food is almost always very reasonably priced and very good. It is usually very spicy but if you ask they will tone it down. Wherever you decide to eat in California you will almost certainly eat well and for much less than you would pay for the equivalent meal at home.

Mexican Cuisine

Nowhere outside Mexico is there such a concentration of Mexican restaurants. There is hardly a town in the state that does not have at least one.

There is no better place to go for a meal that is both filling and inexpensive. The staple ingredients of Mexican food are beans, corn and rice, and though it never quite reaches the elevated heights of *haute cuisine,* occasionally a restaurant will go beyond the usual offerings to provide a more imaginative menu. Some 90 per cent of the restaurants, however, all serve variations of the same dishes.

This is good, hearty food of the people and should be approached on that level.

All meals start with a basket of tortilla chips, also called corn chips. Corn is the American name for maize, the most widely used grain in Mexican cooking.

The chips are accompanied by salsa, a mixture of tomatoes, onions, chillies and cilantro (coriander) which can vary between mild and painfully hot.

This, usually complimentary, starter is a great thirst creator and Mexican food is best when washed down with cold beer or margaritas. Mexican brands of beer include Dos Equis, Bohemia and Tecate.

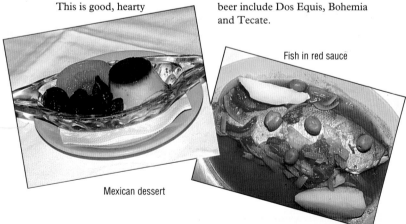

Fish in red sauce

Mexican dessert

Tequila is a potent distilled spirit made from the agave plant, and the hangovers it can induce are legendary! Mixed with triple sec, lime juice and ice it becomes a margarita. It will always be served with salt around the rim of the glass unless you specify otherwise.

A menu reader
A knowledge of these basic dishes will steer you through any Mexican menu.

Chile rellenos
Green chilies stuffed with cheese and deep-fried in egg batter.

Chimichangas
fried tortillas filled with beef or chicken

Chorizo
spicy Mexican sausage

Enchiladas
lightly fried tortillas filled with shredded beef, chicken or cheese

Guacamole
avocado dip

Mole
pronounced molay, is a piquant sauce often, but not always, made with chocolate.

Tamales
maize dough cooked in the maize husk

Tostada
a crisp, fried tortilla heaped with lettuce and either beef or chicken

All main dishes are usually served with refried beans, rice, guacamole and our cream.

Fast Food
The Mexican equivalent of the hamburger is the burrito, a pancake made from maize flour, called a tortilla, and filled with shredded beef or chicken, refried beans and cheese. A taco is a crispy, deep-fried tortilla filled with shredded lettuce and beef or chicken.

The two most widespread fast-food chains are **Taco Bell** and **El Polo Loco**.

Mexican cocktail

Guacamole

Hotels and Accommodation

*C*alifornia has an enormous variety of choice of accommodation, from budget to super-luxury, and it is all comparatively inexpensive compared with much of the rest of the world.

It is also of an almost universally high standard. Even the cheapest places are clean and well appointed. This does not include inner-city residential hotels which cater for transients and often look as though they went out of business decades ago.

MOTELS

The motel, of course, is the American lodging *par excellence*. For the budget-conscious traveller, these are by far the best places to stay. They can be unbelievably cheap and they are never very expensive.

The chain motels are perhaps the most predictable for quality but they fill up quickly so it pays to book ahead. They all provide a clean, simply decorated room, usually with the choice of twin or double beds. There is always a television, a telephone in all but the most

The Bonaventure, Los Angeles

basic, and always a bathroom or shower and toilet *en suite*.

The difference between the cheapest and the next category up is very slight. There may be a swimming pool and you may get a sachet of shampoo in the bathroom but these refinements can cost $20– $30 more without any basic increase in comfort. Payment is usually in advance and rooms will be held only until 5pm unless the reservation is secured with a credit card.

Motels tend to be on the outskirts of town on the main roads, and are rarely in the best locations for sightseeing. If you have a car this should not present a problem. Motels are usually very well advertised with huge roadside signs. Most towns have a motel strip; in San Francisco it is Lombard Street, and any local should be able to tell you where to go.

Breakfast is never included but there is usually a restaurant close by and vending machines for soft drinks. Complimentary coffee is sometimes provided in reception (lobby in US) Good, very inexpensive chains are:

Motel 6 *(tel: 800 437 7486)*
Days Inn *(tel: 800 325 2525)*
Super 8 *(tel: 800 800 8000)*
Also very good but not as cheap are:
Travelodge *(tel: 800 255 3050)*
Comfort Inn *(tel: 800 221 2222)*
Vagabond Inn *(tel: 800 522 1555)*
Best Western *(tel: 800 528 1234)*
Howard Johnson's *(tel: 800 654 2000)*
(All these numbers are toll-free.)

Full-service hotels are much more expensive than motels and they are generally only found in the major cities.

STAYING IN STYLE

Some of the great classic hotels of the world are here for those who can afford

The Hyatt Regent, San Francisco

them. For the ultimate in both luxury and service these are the places to stay:
In San Diego: the Hotel del Coronado and the Valencia
In Los Angeles: the Biltmore, Beverly Wilshire, Bel Air and Beverly Hills Hotel
In San Francisco: the Fairmont, the Mark Hopkins, Westin St Francis and Four Seasons – Clift
In Santa Barbara: the Biltmore
In Yosemite: the Ahwahnee

Even in hotels of this quality breakfast is rarely included in the price although there is a growing trend to include a continental breakfast at some hotels.

Also at the top end of the market are resort hotels that not only provide de luxe service and surroundings, but also a range of sports, including tennis and golf, and often spa facilities. Once you have checked into one of these luxury resorts there is no reason to set foot in the outside world again until your money runs out.

Some of the best are:
La Costa near San Diego
Ritz-Carlton at Laguna Niguel
La Quinta near Rancho Mirage
Lodge at Pebble Beach
Meadowood Resort in Napa Valley
Sonoma Mission Inn and **Spa**
Claremont Resort in Berkeley

Most of the big international hotel chains have properties in California and these provide a more reasonably priced alternative without the glamour of a landmark building. They are usually well located near main tourist attractions.
Hilton *(tel: 800 445 8667)*
Hyatt *(tel: 800 228 9000)*
Sheraton *(tel: 800 325 3535)*
Ramada *(tel: 800 272 6232)*
Holiday Inn *(tel: 800 465 4329)*
Marriot *(tel: 800 228 9290)*
Doubletree *(tel: 800 528 0444)*
(All these numbers are toll-free)

BED AND BREAKFAST
Northern California has a growing number of bed and breakfast inns. You can find them in Carmel, San Francisco, Napa Valley, the Gold Country and Mendocino. Do not be deceived. These are not the budget seaside accommodations of Europe. In California they can be more expensive than some hotels. There are all superbly appointed and usually very romantic. The Victorian motif of most of these places is a big selling point with Californians who are hungry for history, however recent.

For a list of inns in California send a SAE to **Bed and Breakfast International**, *151 Ardmore Road, Kensington, CA 94707*.
If writing from outside the US, enclose an International Reply Coupon.

Holiday Inn, downtown San Francisco

The Achilles Heel, Haight Street

GETTING THE BEST VALUE

When making reservations for any accommodation make sure it is in a convenient location. Ask plenty of questions. It is also worth asking if there are any special rates available. Many places will give significant discounts rather than lose the business; it never does any harm to ask.

Several chains offer discounts if vouchers are purchased outside the US. These include:

Howard Johnson's Freedom North America, Vagabond Discover America Hotel Pass, and Tourcheck America who handle bookings for Best Western, Hilton, Holiday Inn, Ramada, Travelodge and Quality Inn hotels and motels.

Most travel agents should be aware of these programmes and have vouchers available for purchase.

Long-distance calls from in-room telephones can be marked up by quite outrageous amounts and there is often a charge for just using the phone for reverse charge (collect) or credit card calls. Always find out what these charges are to avoid a nasty shock when it is too late. All hotels and motels have public telephones available in the lobby areas. Many hotels do not charge for local calls but, paradoxically, it is usually the cheaper places that have this policy. Again, check before use.

In-room mini-bars are another big profit centre for hotels. Drinks are so cheap in California that if you enjoy a nightcap it is almost as cheap to buy a full bottle at a supermarket as it is to buy a miniature from a mini-bar.

HOSTELS

Very low-cost accommodation is available in both YMCA/YWCA hostels (known as 'Y') or in Youth Hostels (AYH). The 'Ys' are only found in larger cities but the 'AYHs' are located in most tourist centres and hiking areas.

A complete listing can be found in the International Youth Hostel Handbook or contact **American Youth Hostel Association**, *P O Box 37613, Washington DC 20013.*
For information on YMCAs look in the telephone directory.

Practical Guide

ARRIVING

Los Angeles International is the main airport for international flights into southern California, handling over 60 airlines; San Diego is smaller and it is used by some international charter companies. San Francisco International serves northern California, with Oakland and San Jose handling some charter flights.

Domestic flights are generally very expensive with the exception of the services between San Francisco and Los Angeles. If planning short hops within the state or flying in from another state, it is advisable to purchase a ticket before arrival. Several airliners offer Visit USA passes, and travel agents should be able to advise on the best deals.

Virtually all California's commercial airports have all the facilities a traveller would expect, although only the major airports will have banking facilities. Disabled travellers are usually well provided for. Services available for business travellers include conference rooms and a wide range of communications facilities.

At both Los Angeles International and San Francisco International there is a wide range of choice for transport into town. There are several car rental companies, taxis and buses. Airporters offer a door-to-door service for significantly less than a taxi but take longer as they carry several passengers and make frequent stops. Most major hotels in the vicinity of the airports offer a free shuttle service.

Airport taxes are included in the price of the ticket.

Passports are required by all visitors to the USA, visas are required by all visitors except Canadians, New Zealanders and UK citizens visiting for business or tourism for a stay of not more than 90 days, and providing that an onward or return ticket is held and that they are arriving in the USA on a 'participating carrier'. UK citizens and New Zealanders must also have completed a visa waiver form. Whilst in the USA the visitors can take a side trip overland or by sea to Canada or Mexico and re-enter the USA without a visa within the 90 day period. This rule also applies to nationals of Andorra, Belgium, Netherlands, Luxembourg, Denmark, Finland, France, Germany, Iceland, Italy, Japan, Liechtenstein,

Airport shuttle services are cheap

Monaco, Norway, San Marino, Spain, Sweden, Switzerland. Immigration laws are strictly enforced and it is advisable to check with the American Embassy well before departure.

Major Airline Telephone Numbers
Air Canada *(tel: 800 776 3000)*
Air New Zealand *(tel: 800 262 1234)*
American Airlines *(tel: 800 433 7300)*
British Airways *(tel: 800 247 9297)*
Continental Airlines *(tel: 800 322 8662)*
Delta Air Lines *(tel: 800 221 1212)*
Northwest Airlines *(tel: 800 225 2525)*
Trans World Airlines *(tel: 800 221 2000)*
Quantas *(tel: 800 227 4500)*
USAIR *(tel: 800 842 5374)*
United Express *(tel: 800 241 6522)*
(All these numbers are toll-free)

CAMPING
The California climate lends itself to camping holidays and outside the major cities there is no shortage of camp sites.

National and state parks have excellent camping facilities but reservations must be made during the peak season. This is the summer for most of the state and winter for the deserts. Some parks impose 7 to 15 day limits during these periods. Reservations

at state parks can be made through:
Reservations, Department of Parks and Recreation, *Box 942896, Sacramento, California 94296–0001 (tel: 916 445 6477).*
For national parks camp sites contact:
National Park Service, *Fort Mason, Building 201, San Francisco CA 94123 (tel: 415 556 0560).*

Some of the best camp sites are in California's 18 National Forests. Reservations can be made up to 120 days in advance by telephoning *800 283 2267* toll-free. For information on the camp sites contact: **USDA Forest Service,** *630 Sansome Street, San Francisco CA 94111 (tel: 415 556 0122).*

Back country camping is allowed in the national parks but wilderness permits must first be obtained from the park. Bears can be a serious problem and there are strict rules concerning storage of food. Never ignore the warnings and rules laid down by the park service.

There are many private camp sites that generally have more sophisticated facilities than those in the parks. They cater particularly for camper vans and motor homes, providing both water and electricity hook ups. A directory on private campgrounds is available from: **California Travel Parks Association,** *PO BOX 5648, Auburn, CA 95604 (tel: 916 885 1624).*

On-site tent hire is not generally available but equipment can be bought inexpensively from sports shop chains.

Camper vans are available for hire in major towns. In the US they are called motor homes and they are not available from regular car hire sources. One of the biggest companies is Cruise America *(tel: 800 327 7778 toll-free).* Local firms are listed under 'Motor Home – Renting and Leasing' in the Yellow Pages.

CHILDREN

Throughout the state children are well catered for. Many hotels provide cots (cribs) at no extra charge, and extra beds for older children are available at a nominal charge. Larger hotels offer babysitting services that are safe and reliable. Many restaurants have children's menus or offer children's portions from the main menu. High chairs are universally available.

Food and nappies (diapers) for infants are available in profusion at any supermarket or drugstore, and in most towns they will be available 24 hours a day from at least one convenience store. Baby milk is called infant formula and is available in several dairy and non-dairy varieties. Prices are very reasonable.

California is generally safe for tourists, but never leave children unattended.

CLIMATE

The best months for travel are generally April to June and September to November. In July and August the temperatures can be sizzling in the deserts of southern California and cold and foggy on the north coast and in San Francisco. December to March is usually wet and cold. During these months, however, the snowfall in the high Sierra provides world-class skiing and when it stops snowing the skies are usually blue.

> **Weather Chart Conversion**
> 25.4mm = 1 inch
> °F = 1.8 × °C + 32

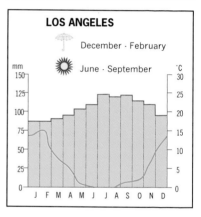

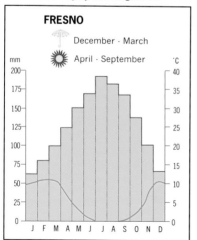

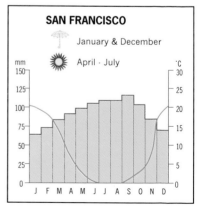

The winter is the best time to visit the deserts, and in March the flowers will be starting to bloom.

CONSULATE GENERALS

Australia
1 Bush Street, 7th Floor,
San Francisco, CA 94104
(tel: 415 362 6160)
611 N. Larchmont Boulevard,
Los Angeles, CA 90004
(tel: 213 469 4300)

Canada
50 Fremont Street, Suit 2100,
San Francisco, CA 94105
(tel: 414 495 7030)
300 South Grand Avenue, 10th Floor,
Los Angeles, CA 90071
(tel: 213 687 7432)

Ireland
655 Montgomery Street,
San Francisco, CA
(tel: 415 392 4214)

New Zealand
10960 Wilshire Boulevard, Suite 1530,
Los Angeles, CA 90024
(tel: 213 477 8241)

United Kingdom
Ahmanson Center, East Building,
Suite 312, 3701 Wilshire Boulevard,
Los Angeles, CA 90010
(tel: 213 385 7381)
1 Sansome Street, Suite 850,
San Francisco, CA 94104
(tel: 415 981 3030)

CRIME

Crime is a very real problem but should be put into perspective. It is at its worst in the big cites but not really any worse than many other major cities throughout the world.

General availability of handguns is one of the major problems but the chances of even seeing a gun, other than on a policeman's hip, is very remote. Most shootings are in areas that tourists would rarely visit. However, it is unwise to get into a confrontational situation with anyone, particularly while driving. Frayed tempers have often been known to result in shootings. It is also unwise to pick up hitch-hikers.

A more real problem is theft, both from cars and hotel rooms. Take sensible precautions and make sure valuables are not blatantly on display. Most hotel thefts are opportunist, and the more difficult it is to snatch something and run the less chance it will be stolen.

It is wise to carry travellers' cheques rather than cash. All hotels and most shops and restaurants will accept US Dollar cheques which can be purchased before leaving home. Thomas Cook, Visa and American Express traveller's cheques are widely recognised. In the event of loss or theft, Thomas Cook traveller's cheques can be refunded quickly and efficiently at one of the many refund points listed on p183. You can also contact the Thomas Cook Refund Service by telephone, 24 hours a day, 365 days a year. Both VISA and American Express also provide fast service in the case of loss or theft.

Shopping is usually trouble-free. Prices for consumer goods in the US are generally much better than other parts of the world but care should be taken in some tourist areas, particularly with cameras and electronic goods. Buy an appropriate magazine and look at the small ads in the back. You may not be able to equal the prices you find there, which are often for New York stores, but it will give you a good idea of the general range.

Good protection can be obtained if

you pay by credit card. If the goods are unsatisfactory the charge can often be disputed with the credit card company.

CUSTOMS REGULATIONS

Everyone entering the US must pass through US customs. Personal allowances for visitors include one quart (0.9461litres) of spirits or wine, 300 cigarettes or 50 cigars plus up to $100 worth of gifts. In practice, most of these items are far cheaper within the US than at airport duty free shops so there is little point importing them.

There is no restriction on the amount of currency imported or exported but anything over $10,000 must be declared.

US customs are particularly concerned about drugs, animals, meat (both fresh and processed), plants and fresh fruit. Penalties are severe.

DISABLED TRAVELLERS

California is more responsive to the needs of the disabled than many places.

At airports there are always good facilities including special lifts, toilets and availability of wheelchairs.

Most hotels, public buildings and museums now have wheelchair access and toilet facilities. Any public building erected or renovated since 1982 is required by law to have extensive facilities for the disabled, including access and toilets. It is always a good idea to check with your destination to verify that adequate facilities are available.

Handicapped parking areas are widely available and hefty fines are given for illegal use of these spaces. They are always marked in blue and with a wheelchair symbol.

Throughout the state people will be sympathetic to the problems of the disabled and generally very helpful.

DRIVING

Accidents

1 Set up warning signs. Flares are usually used in California and are available from any auto store.
2 Call police and an ambulance if required. The emergency telephone number is 911.
3 Take the names and addresses of all involved, make and licence plates of the other vehicle, and the names and numbers of insurance policies.
4 Write down names and addresses of any witnesses, together with the time and date of the accident. If possible take photographs of the accident from several angles.
5 Under no circumstance admit to or sign any statement of responsibility.

Breakdown

The American Automobile Association (AAA) is a member of a worldwide association of motoring organisations (AIT) and as such makes certain services available to visitors of member organisations. The Triple A operates a nationwide road service number *(tel: 1-800-AAA-HELP)* which will give you information on obtaining emergency assistance. Should you break down on a highway lift up the bonnet (hood) of your car and remain in the vehicle until the Highway Patrol arrives. Do not open your doors or windows to anyone else.

Car Hire

Every airport, however small, will have at least one car rental company associated with it. The major airports have several. All the major companies are represented (Hertz, Avis, Budget, National and Dollar) but there are hundreds of local companies that often offer better rates. Generally, off-airport companies offer the best value and they all provide a free shuttle service to their facility. There are dozens of listings in the Yellow Pages.

It is usually better to arrange for a car before arriving. Several airlines have special deals available with preferential rates if the booking is made in advance. It is always better to make a reservation if possible as certain categories of car may be in short supply during peak seasons.

Automatic transmission is standard on all rental cars. American cars are big and a so-called mid-size is huge by European standards. The smallest size available is the sub-compact which will just carry 4 people and a small amount of luggage. For summer travel, ask for a car with air-conditioning. It should be available at no extra cost.

None of the major car rental companies will rent to anyone under the age of 25. It may be possible to find a local company that will, but be prepared to pay a loaded insurance premium.

Extra collision insurance will always be offered and this can be almost 50 per cent of the rental fee. You may already be covered by your own personal car insurance policy. Check before leaving home.

In cases of breakdown immediately inform the car rental company and await instructions.

Documentation

Drivers will need a valid licence from any country signatory to the 1949 Geneva Agreement. International Driver's Permits are generally unnecessary.

Major roads are well surfaced and well signed.

Alfresco in Frisco

Driving Tips

Americans drive on the right-hand side of the road. Because of the low speed limits, freeway driving is generally safe. In cities there is a continual problem with drivers anticipating traffic lights or trying to make it through on amber. Always be careful at these junctions.

There are many minor junctions where there is a stop sign in only one direction and they are often not clearly marked. Pay particular attention when driving off the main roads. Road signs use international symbols.

In Los Angeles it is wise to plan your journey ahead of time. The freeways can be so complicated that a missed turn-off can result in a lot of frustration and lost time.

Petrol

California is a car-oriented state and there is no shortage of petrol stations and garage facilities. Petrol, called gas, is available in one grade in the leaded version for older cars and as regular or super in unleaded. All hire cars will use unleaded. Diesel is also available at most gas stations.

All gas stations have good maps for sale and most car rental companies will have local maps available free of charge. The main motoring organisation in the US is the American Automobile Association (AAA or the Triple A). The Association has reciprocal agreements with overseas motoring organisations and both roadside assistance and free route maps are available upon presentation of your membership card.

Speed Limits

Motorways are called freeways and other roads are highways. The speed limit in all highways and freeways is 55mph unless otherwise posted. It is 65mph on rural freeways. In town the limit is between 25 and 35mph. Speed limits are well signposted and strictly enforced. On freeways you can theoretically be ticketed for driving too slowly in the left hand lane, but this rarely happens.

ELECTRICITY

The standard supply is 110 volts at 60 cycles.

Adapters are readily available for purchase in the US but it may be easier to bring one from home to save time finding a shop that sells them.

EMERGENCY TELEPHONE NUMBERS

For police, fire and ambulance dial 911
Thomas Cook traveller's cheques loss or theft: *1-800-223-7373 (Freephone)*
The Thomas Cook bureaux listed on p183 can give emergency assistance.

HEALTH

There are no specific health requirement for visitors to California.

The standard of health care is extremely high but so are the costs, and it is essential to have a good insurance policy. Many doctors and hospitals will refuse to give treatment unless proof of insurance can be given. All major hospitals have 24-hour emergency rooms.

Information on doctors can be obtained from hotels or listings in the Yellow Pages.

California does not have many specific health problems. Tap water is drinkable but if hiking in the back country do not drink water from the streams which often carries the parasite *Giardia*.

AIDS is a continuing concern, particularly in the San Francisco area where the AIDS Hotline telephone number is *415 863 2437*. Needless to say, safe sex is an absolute necessity.

HITCH-HIKING

Hitch-hiking is only illegal on freeways. However, it is not recommended in California. Motorists are very wary of hitch-hikers.

INSURANCE

Travel insurance to cover both loss of property and medical expenses is highly recommended. Make sure that medical policies give adequate cover, including emergency flights home.

Cancellation insurance is advisable if appropriate.

LAUNDRY

All major hotels have one-day laundry and dry cleaning services from Monday to Friday.

Alternatively, there are may dry-cleaning shops offering a two- to four-hour service. Check Yellow Pages.

MAPS

General maps are available from car hire companies. More detailed town maps and walking maps are usually available free of charge at Chambers of Commerce or Visitor Bureaux which will be listed in the telephone Yellow Pages. For AAA maps see Driving on pages 178–179. Detailed trekking maps are on sale in the National Park visitor centres.

MEASUREMENTS AND SIZES

California still uses the imperial system of measurement.

Conversion Table

FROM	TO	MULTIPLY BY
Inches	Centimetres	2.54
Centimetres	Inches	0.3937
Feet	Metres	0.3048
Metres	Feet	3.2808
Yards	Metres	0.9144
Metres	Yards	1.0940
Miles	Kilometres	1.6090
Kilometres	Miles	0.6214
Acres	Hectares	0.4047
Hectares	Acres	2.4710
Gallons (UK)	Litres	4.5460
Litres	Gallons (UK)	0.2200
Gallons (US)	Litres	3.7854
Litres	Gallons (US)	0.2642
Ounces	Grams	28.35
Grams	Ounces	0.0353
Pounds	Grams	453.6
Grams	Pounds	0.0022
Pounds	Kilograms	0.4536
Kilograms	Pounds	2.205
Tons	Tonnes	1.0160
Tonnes	Tons	0.9842

Cable car tour of downtown San Francisco

Men's Suits

UK		36	38	40	42	44	46	48
Rest of Europe	46	48	50	52	54	56	58
US		36	38	40	42	44	46	48

Dress Sizes

UK	8	10	12	14	16	18
France	36	38	40	42	44	46
Italy	38	40	42	44	46	48
Rest of Europe	34	36	38	40	42	44
US	6	8	10	12	14	16

Men's Shirts

UK	14	14.5	15	15.5	16	16.5	17
Rest of Europe	36	37	38	39/40	41	42	43
US	14	14.5	15	15.5	16	16.5	17

Men's Shoes

UK	7	7.5	8.5	9.5	10.5	11
Rest of Europe	41	42	43	44	45	46
US	8	8.5	9.5	10.5	11.5	12

Women's Shoes

UK	4.5	5	5.5	6	6.5	7
Rest of Europe	38	38	39	39	40	41
US	6	6.5	7	7.5	8	8.5

MEDIA

The closest there is to a national daily newspaper in California is the *Los Angeles Times*. In northern California the *San Francisco Chronicle* is the morning daily and the *Examiner* the afternoon daily, but both tend to be rather parochial. In most towns you can find both the *Wall Street Journal* and the *New York Times*, which often give a more global view of the news.

For local news, including weather and traffic conditions, keep the car radio tuned to one of the news stations. There is a radio station for virtually every interest from classical to rap and including what is know as 'talk attract calls' from the fringes of society and are usually banal at best. They can, however, provide an amusing diversion and provide an insight into the American psyche.

In most parts of the state it is possible to receive a Public Broadcasting Service (PBS) station. The quality of programming is considerably more intelligent than the other networks and they carry the BBC News.

Virtually every hotel and motel room in the state will have a television. More often than not it will be cable TV offering 30 or more channels. The problem is finding one worth watching. As with radio there are usually two or three PBS stations which give good news coverage, even if most of the other programmes are second-hand from British TV.

The newspapers all carry full TV guides, but there are no radio listings and you just have to keep trying until you find a station you like.

MONEY MATTERS

Banking hours have traditionally been from 10am–3pm Monday to Friday but recent competition has resulted in longer opening hours and even Saturday opening. There is no longer a general rule, except that the 10–3 core period is the same.

Most banks do not offer foreign exchange facilities but it is possible to exchange money at the airport or hotel. Thomas Cook traveller's cheques can be cashed free of commission charges at the Thomas Cook locations listed below. If denominated in dollars they can be used

San Francisco souvenirs

as cash in most shops, hotels and restaurants.

Thomas Cook bureaux de change are located at:

Orange County: The City Shopping Centre, 8 City Boulevard East, Suite 83, Orange (Mon–Sat).
Newport Fashion Island, 1113 Newport Centre Drive, Newport Beach (Mon–Sun).
South Coast Plaza, 3333 N. Bristol Street, Suite 1417, Costa Mesa (Mon–Sun).

San Diego: 177 Horton Plaza, San Diego (Mon–Sat).
University Towne Centre, 4525 La Jolla Village Drive, Suite D1B (Mon–Sat).

Los Angeles: 452 North Bedford Drive, Beverly Hills (Mon–Sat).
Bank of Los Angeles, 8901 Santa Monica Boulevard, West Hollywood (Mon–Fri).

San Francisco: The Village at Corte Madera, 1512 Redwood Highway, Corte Madera (Mon–Sat).
75 Geary Street (Mon–Sat).
San Francisco Intl. Airport, Departures Level, International Terminal (Mon–Sat).

It is useful to have small-denomination cheques when using them as cash.

The US dollar bill is available in denominations of 1, 5, 10, 20, 50 and 100. There is a two-dollar bill but it is rarely seen. Be very careful, as all notes are exactly the same size and same colour. It is better to avoid the higher denomination to avoid expensive mistakes. Coins come in denominations of 1 (penny), 5 (nickel), 10 (dime), 25

Colorado Boulevard, Los Angeles

(quarter). Always keep a few quarters (25 cents) handy for parking meters, telephones and newspapers.

All major credit cards are universally accepted.

Sales tax is applied to all goods and restaurant meals within California, and an additional 7–8.5 per cent (depending upon the county) will be added to the price tag.

There are no restrictions on the amount of money that can be either brought into or taken out of the US (see Customs Regulations).

NATIONAL AND STATE HOLIDAYS

New Year's Day *(1 January)*
Martin Luther King Day *(3rd Monday in January)*
Lincoln's Birthday *(12 February)*
Washington's Birthday *(3rd Monday in February)*
Memorial Day *(last Monday in May)*
Independence Day *(4 July)*
Labor Day *(1st Monday in September)*
Admission Day *(9 September)*
Columbus Day *(2nd Monday in October)*
Veteran's Day *(11 November)*
Thanksgiving *(4th Thursday in November)*
Christmas *(25 December)*

All aboard for a sightseeing tour

Government offices, including post offices, are closed for most of these holidays, but few people observe them all. Shops remain open on all but Thanksgiving and Christmas. Peak periods for travel, hotels and camp sites are Memorial Day, Independence Day and Labor Day. Air travel peaks at Thanksgiving and Christmas.

OPENING HOURS

Most larger shops are open seven days a week, typically from 10am to 6pm and from noon on Sundays. Smaller shops and more specialised businesses close on Sundays.

Most offices, including government offices, open Monday to Friday, 9am–5pm.

Museums and art galleries vary dramatically. Recent budget deficits have resulted in severely curtailed opening hours at many state museums, and it is always wise to check before a visit.

ORGANISED TOURS

The majority of people visiting California hire cars, which is undoubtedly the best way to see the state. If time is limited a tour may be the best solution. Particularly in cities, tours can remove the headache of searching for parking spaces, and will also ensure that all the major sites are covered.

There are both regular and specialised tours available in the three major cities. If time is limited a regular tour may fit the bill, but it will be with a large bus-load of tourists on a fairly superficial trip. The specialised tours cater for specific interests and are usually with smaller groups of people.

Dozens of tour operators serve California, and hotels will usually be able to give advice on what is available.

Regular sightseeing tours of Los Angeles, San Francisco and San Diego are given by **Gray Line**, the largest operator of its type in the state. They are reliable and comprehensive but they are with large, impersonal groups. Gray Line do, however, offer the widest range of general tours.

Los Angeles *(tel: 213 481 2121)*
San Francisco *(tel: 415 558 7300)*
San Diego *(tel: 619 231 9922)*

Specialised tours

Cable Car Charter's motorised cable cars pick up passengers every half hour from Pier 41 in San Francisco for either a Heart of San Francisco or Golden Gate Bridge tour. The tour is very basic but the transportation is interesting, even if not authentic *(tel: 800 562 7383 toll-free)*.

The **California Native** offers trips to the mountains and deserts just outside Los Angeles and includes Old West historical sites and San Andreas Fault. They offer several one-day and weekend getaways that include whale-watching and caving. Reservations must be made well in advance: *6701 West 87th Place, Los Angeles CA 90045 (tel: 213 642 1140)*.

Grave Line Tours offers to 'bring to life 100 years of Hollywood's most famous death, sin and scandal'. This 30-mile tour of 'movieland morbidity' is given in a Cadillac hearse and includes two maps to the 'Cemeteries of the Stars'. Reservations are required.
Tel: 213 469 3127 for information
Tel: 213 469 4149 for reservations

PHARMACIES

Most pharmacies are open from at least 9am until 6pm and many have longer hours. Drugstores will have a pharmacy counter for dispensing prescriptions and these are usually open until 9pm. Drugstores are like mini-supermarkets and have a wide range of products on sale including wine and spirits, hardware and snacks.

Yellow Pages gives a compete list of pharmacies.

Many non-prescription drugs can be obtained from regular supermarkets.

PLACES OF WORSHIP

It seems that every religion known to mankind has a place of worship in California.

The state is predominantly Catholic and every neighbourhood has a Catholic church.

Newspapers generally list times of services for the main denominations, and a compete list can be found under 'Churches' in Yellow Pages. In the San Francisco area alone there are 10 pages of churches. This blanket listing covers mosques and Buddhist temples but not synagogues, which have their own listing.

POLICE

Every incorporated city in California has its own police force with normal police responsibilities including traffic control. An incorporated city can have a population as small as 500, though the average is 2,300.

The areas outside the cities are policed by the county sheriff, a different title but essentially the same job except that they have no jurisdiction over traffic. That is the function of the California Highway Patrol. In the case of any emergency throughout the state the telephone number to call is 911.

Green and yellow National taxi cab

POST OFFICES

Post offices are generally open Monday to Friday from 9am to 5pm. They are always closed on Sundays.

Stamps are available from vending machines in some hotels and shops but they will cost more than from a post office. Postage rates change frequently, so always check on current tariffs.

An airmail letter or postcard takes about one week to travel from California to Europe. Surface mail can take three months! Parcels must be properly packaged and, if being sent by registered mail, non-removable, non-shiny tape must be used. Appropriate containers are sold at the post office. A customs declaration form must accompany any parcel being mailed abroad.

Post Restante is known as 'General Delivery'. Letters can be addressed to any post office and must include the zip code.

Mail will only be held for 30 days, after which it will be returned to the sender, whose name and address must be on the envelope.

When collecting general delivery mail you will need some form of identification.

Post boxes are called mail boxes and are blue with 'US Mail' in white lettering.

Telegrams are sent from Western Union Offices, not from post offices. If you have a credit card you can dictate a telegram over the telephone and charge it. Western Union Offices are listed in Yellow Pages.

PUBLIC TRANSPORT

The majority of Californians drive cars and outside San Francisco the public transportation system, with the exception of air travel, is not well developed.

By Air

All the main towns in California have commercial airports. Between San Francisco (SFO) and Los Angeles (LAX) there are flights virtually every half-hour on several different airlines. Other destinations have much less frequent services. The SFO–LAX route is like a bus service with reasonably priced tickets. Other routes are much more expensive, and it is usually better to buy tickets before arriving in the US.

The whole airline business is in such a state of flux that only a travel agent will be able to give current, comprehensive information on flights and fares.

By Bus

Bus travel is cheap but the distances are so great that, unless your budget is really tight, it wastes valuable time. An additional problem is that the long-distance bus stations tend to be in the less desirable parts of town. Some of the

Signpost on the 49-Mile Drive

passengers on these buses can also leave a lot to be desired. You would not want to share a football stadium with some of the characters who use these buses, never mind a seat.

Greyhound is a major operator travelling between all the main cities. On some routes such as Los Angeles–San Francisco, Greyhound is not significantly cheaper than the cheapest air ticket. For the greatest saving buy an Ameripass which is available for 7, 15 and 30 days and must be purchased outside the US. In London the Greyhound office is at *14–16 Cockspur Street, SW1 (tel: 071 839 5591)*. Local offices in California can be found in Yellow Pages.

An alternative to Greyhound is Green Tortoise which runs weekly trips between Los Angeles and San Francisco at a very reasonable price. It caters particularly for students and younger people. In Los Angeles the telephone number is *213 392 1990* and in San Francisco *415 821 0803*.

By Train
The rail system in California is not well developed. However, all major cites are connected, and Amtrak trains are clean and comfortable if not particularly fast.

Discount rail passes are available at Amtrak stations in Los Angeles and San Francisco on the production of your passport.

Other Transport
Taxis are available in all towns of any size but are quite expensive.

In San Francisco, cable car rides are a must but these days they are as much a tourist attraction as a means of transport. Only three lines are now in operation (see **San Francisco**).

The Bay Area Rapid Transit

In the San Francisco Bay area The Bay Area Rapid Transit (BART) provides a fast, efficient underground train service between San Francisco and the East Bay. It links 8 city stations with 25 in the East Bay in a 71-mile network.

The ferries are the most pleasant way to travel across the bay. The Red and White fleet *((tel: 800 445 8880 toll-fee)* operates between San Francisco, Angel Island, Tiburon and Vallejo. The Golden Gate Ferry Service *(415 332 6600)* operates between San Francisco and Sausalito.

In San Diego the 'Tijuana trolley' makes the 16-mile journey to the Mexican border every 15 minutes throughout the day and links several San Diego communities.

SENIOR CITIZENS
Most hotels, motels, restaurants and museums have preferential rates for senior citizens. Usually they want to see some form of identification but often just looking old enough will work (which can be very demoralising!).

SMOKING

California, always a leader in social trends, has almost banned smoking. It is not allowed on public transport nor in any public buildings. Smoking is not permitted in offices either.

Many hotels offer non-smoking rooms and car hire companies offer smoke-free cars.

An increasing number of restaurants are banning smoking completely

Smokers are generally looked upon as social pariahs and they are rapidly becoming the exception rather than the rule in California.

TELEPHONES

In California telephones are everywhere and most of them work. Apart from telephone kiosks there are public telephones in most bars, restaurants and hotel lobbies. You are never far from a phone.

All public telephones accept 5, 10

Although the queues can be lengthy, buy your ticket before you get in

and 25 cent coins, with 25 cents being the minimum change. In airports there are often telephones that allow the call to be charged to a credit card.

Hotels usually charge a high premium for calls from rooms. Conversely, some hotels allow local calls at no cost. Always check the rates to avoid an unpleasant surprise when checking out.

Reverse charge calls, called collect calls, can be made from any telephone by calling the operator. Dial 0 for the local operator or 00 for a long-distance operator.

All numbers with an 800 prefix are toll-free. At a public telephone insert a dime first (10c) which will be returned when you hang up.

For international calls dial 001, the country code and then the number. The cheapest time for transatlantic calls is between 11pm and 7am.

International codes are:

Australia	61
Canada	no country code from US
Ireland	353
New Zealand	64
United Kingdom	44
Local directory information:	411
Long-distance directory enquiries (area code):	555 1212

TIME

California is on Pacific Standard Time which is 8 hours behind GMT.

From the last Sunday in April to the first Sunday in October daylight saving time is in operation, when the clocks are put forward by one hour.

TIPPING

Tips are a way of life and everyone in the service industry expects them. They are very rarely included in the bill except occasionally in restaurants when there is a large party. Always check.

The amount is, of course, always at the discretion of the customer but this is a general guide:

Restaurants and bars 15 per cent
Cloakroom attendants $1
Parking valet $1
Airport porters (skycaps) $1 per bag
Taxi drivers 15 per cent
Tour guide or driver $1 per day
Hotel porter $1 per bag
Room maid $2 per day
Hotel parking valet $1
Room service 15 per cent
Hairdresser 10 per cent
Shoe shine 50 cents
Toilet attendant 50 cents

TOILETS

Public toilets, called rest rooms, are not always easy to find but when you do they are almost always clean and free. In cities they can be found in large department stores, bars and restaurants, and all petrol stations.

TOURIST OFFICES

For general information on California contact:

California Office of Tourism, PO Box 9278, Van Nuys, CA 91409 (tel: 800 862 2543 toll-free). They can provide maps, comprehensive brochures and referrals to local Chambers of Commerce for more specific information.

San Diego: San Diego International Visitor Information Center, 11 Horton Plaza, CA 92101 (tel: 619 236 1212).

Written requests for information should be sent to:

San Diego Convention and Visitors Bureau, 1200 Third Avenue, Suite 824, Dept 700, CA 92101.

Orange County: Anaheim Visitor and Convention Bureau, 800 West Katella Avenue, Anaheim, CA 92892 (tel: 714 999 8999).

Joshua Tree National Monument

Happiness is a merry-go-round

Greater Los Angeles Area: Greater Los Angeles Visitor and Information Center, 675 South Figueroa Street, 11th Floor, CA 90017 (tel: 213 689 8822).

Palm Springs Area: Palm Springs Visitor Information Center, 2781 North Palm Canyon Drive, CA 92262 (tel: 800 347 7777 toll-free).

Palm Springs Desert Resorts Conventions and Visitors Bureau, Atrium Design Center, 69–930 Highway 111, Suite 201, Rancho Mirage, CA 92270 (tel: 619 770 9000).

Central Coast: Santa Barbara Conference and Visitors Bureau, 510A State Street, Santa Barbara, CA 93101 (tel: 800 927 4688 toll-free).

San Francisco Bay Area: San Francisco Information Center, Hallidie Plaza, Lower Level, Powell and Market Streets, San Francisco, CA 94101 (tel:

415 391 2000).

Written requests for information should be sent to:
San Francisco Convention and Visitors Bureau, 201 Third Street, Suite 900, San Francisco, CA 94103.

High Sierra: Lake Tahoe Visitors Authority, 1156 Ski Run Boulevard, P O Box 16299, South Lake Tahoe, CA 95706 (tel: 800 288 2463 toll-free).

North Coast: Redwood Empire Association, 785 Market Street, 15th Floor, San Francisco, CA 94103 (tel: 415 543 8334).

Thomas Cook Travel Offices

Orange County: 16735 Von Karman Avenue, Suite 110, Irvine.

San Diego: La Jolla Gateway, 9191 Towne Centre Drive, Suite 170.

Los Angeles: 269 South Lake Avenue, Pasadena; 937 Westwood Boulevard; 111 West Ocean Blvd; and Suite 102, Long Beach.

San Francisco: 425 Market Street, Suite 2840, One Metropolitan Plaza; and Eastridge World Travel, 205 Eastridge Centre, San Jose.

WHAT TO TAKE

Most people find that they take too much to California. You can find everything you can get at home and more, and it is generally cheaper. Clothes are particularly good value. The best advice is to leave plenty of room in your suitcase for the many bargains that you will inevitably want to take home with you.

ACKNOWLEDGEMENTS

The Automobile Association wishes to thank the following organisations, libraries and photographers for their assistance in the preparation of this book.

THE DEPARTMENT OF PARKS & RECREATION OFFICE OF PUBLIC RELATIONS 125; GOLDEN GATE FIELDS 156; MARY EVANS PICTURE LIBRARY 6, 7, 48a; NATURE PHOTOGRAPHERS LTD 72; SPECTRUM COLOUR LIBRARY spine, 14 O, 137; ZEFA PICTURE LIBRARY (UK) LTD cover and inset.

ROBERT HOLMES was commissioned to take the photographs for this book, and the remaining photographs listed below are from the Automobile Associations own picture library (AA PHOTO LIBRARY)

Harold Harris P35, 109a, 109b, 109c, 182; Robert Holmes Title Page, 2, 4a, 4b, 9, 10, 11a, 11b, 12, 13a, 13b, 15, 19, 20, 21a, 21b, 23a, 23b, 27, 29, 31, 37, 39, 41a, 41b, 42, 43, 44, 45, 47, 48b, 48c, 49, 51, 54a, 54b, 54c, 55a, 55b, 56, 58, 59, 60, 63, 65, 66a, 66b, 69, 70, 71, 73a, 73b, 74, 75, 77, 78, 79, 81, 82, 84, 85, 86, 87a, 87b, 88a, 88b, 88c, 89a, 89b, 91, 94, 95, 98a, 98b, 98c, 102, 103, 104, 105, 106, 107, 110, 111, 112, 113, 114a, 114b, 115, 119, 120, 122, 124, 126, 127, 129a, 129b, 129c, 129d, 130, 121, 133, 134, 138, 139, 141, 143a, 143b, 143c, 143d, 145, 146, 154, 155, 157, 158, 159, 160, 161a, 170, 183, 186, 189; Barrie Smith P37, 148, 149, 161b, 163, 166, 167a, 167b, 171, 172, 173, 175, 179, 181, 184, 185, 187, 188

The author would like to thank the following people and institutions for additional help: the California Office of Tourism, the various Visitors and Convention Bureaux through out the state, Maurice and Marjorie Holmes, his wife bobbie and his daughter Emma. The Automobile Association would also like to thank Robyn Mitchell of Thomas Cook Holidays for her help as information consultant.

Series adviser: Melissa Shales